山东大学齐鲁医院文化建设系列丛书

聂会东文集

吕军 曹英娟 编译

Collected Works of
James Boyd Neal

山东大学出版社

图书在版编目(CIP)数据

聂会东文集/吕军,曹英娟编译.—济南:山东大学出版社,2019.3

(山东大学齐鲁医院文化建设系列丛书)

ISBN 978-7-5607-6303-3

Ⅰ.①聂… Ⅱ.①吕… ②曹… Ⅲ.①聂会东—纪念文集 Ⅳ.①K826.2-53

中国版本图书馆 CIP 数据核字(2019)第 044302 号

责任编辑:徐　翔
封面设计:牛　钧

出版发行:山东大学出版社
社　址　山东省济南市山大南路 20 号
邮　编　250100
电　话　市场部(0531)88364466
经　销:新华书店
印　刷:济南新科印务有限公司
规　格:700 毫米×1000 毫米　1/16
13 印张　190 千字
版　次:2019 年 3 月第 1 版
印　次:2019 年 3 月第 1 次印刷
定　价:36.00 元

《山东大学齐鲁医院文化建设系列丛书》编委会

序一

中国现代医学发展史上，有一位载入史册的特殊外籍人士，在他 70 年的人生岁月中，有 40 年是在中国度过的，为中国现代医学的肇端和发展做出了重要的贡献。他就是山东大学齐鲁医院的创始人、山东现代医学教育的主要奠基者，美北长老会传教医师聂会东(James Boyed Neal)。

1883 年，年轻的美北长老会传教医师聂会东携新婚妻子在海上漂泊数月后，踏上了东方神秘古国的土地，千里迢迢来到安逸静谧的海滨小城登州(今山东蓬莱)，任职于登州文会馆，教授化学和生物等课程并主持登州长老会医院的工作。登州长老会医院在他主持期间"日渐发达"。仅从 1888 年一年的统计数据看，登州长老会医院就收治病患 3344 人，其中新增病患 1396 人，住院病患 61 人，做各种手术 209 例(包括肿瘤切除术 7 例)。1890 年，聂会东夫妇奉调济南，负责教会在济南的医疗事务。在他的主持下，原在济南东关兴华街的"文璧医院"得到扩建，并定名为"华美医院"，也就是现在齐鲁医院的前身。这是济南首家西医医院，也是当时分科最全的医院。在聂会东的努力下，华美医院迅速发展成山东第一医院。据统计，1891～1896 年共收治病人 87766 人次，1894～1896 年开展各种手术计 446 台次。1895 年医院又附设女子医院，以妇产、小儿科为主，并接受产妇住院分娩，有产床 15 张。1911～1912 年，山东肺鼠疫大流行，聂会东因在拯救患者和控制疫情上做出的重大贡献，被中国政府授予"仓廪"(the order of "Garnered Grain")勋章。在长达数十年的医学生涯中，聂会东行医办院，济世活人，其精湛的医术、高尚的医德，赢得了业内同仁和黎民百姓的广泛赞誉。

聂会东非常重视医学教育，对山东乃至全国的现代医学教育系统化、规模化贡献尤多。早在主持登州长老会医院工作期间，他就招收了 5 名学生，采用自己编译的教材，向他们传授西方医学知识，使之成为助手服务病患。1894 年，由聂会东主持的华美医院医校宣告成立。到 1902 年，华美医校就有了 4 个班，22 名学生。同年，英国浸礼会和美北长老会决定合办“山东基督教共合大学”。这所大学分为文理科、神学科和医科，各科分布在省内不同地区。其中，分处济南、青州、邹平、临沂四地的四所教会医学堂合并在济南办学称为“共合医道学堂”。1911 年，济南共合医道学堂更名为“山东基督教共合大学医科”，聂会东任科长。1917 年，在“山东基督教联合大学”的基础上，齐鲁大学成立，聂会东继续担任“齐鲁大学医科”的科长，1919～1921 年，聂会东还担任了齐鲁大学的校长。

作为一名医生、医学教育工作者、管理者，聂会东在行医和教学之余撰写、译介了大量的理论文章、专著和工作报告。2010 年，我们的一位访问学者在耶鲁大学图书馆、美国费城长老会总部图书馆、约翰霍普金斯大学档案馆发现、搜集、整理了这些弥足珍贵的史料。这些史料的获得无疑将对山东乃至中国现代医学史的研究提供较大帮助。

为了表达对这位齐鲁现代医学的奠基者、开创者应有的敬意，同时也为了进一步理清齐鲁现代医学的发展脉络，我们从这些史料中拣选、翻译了 25 篇文章编辑成书，名之为《聂会东文集》。

聂氏虽初学金融后为医学，观其一生，为医则医德高尚、医术精湛；品其文集，行文则含英咀华、笔走龙蛇。文集所录之 25 篇文章，既有阐微发凡之临床研究，又有理法赅备之医案医话，更有诠释其教育理念、办学思想的智慧结晶。古人云：医乃仁术，非精不能明其理，非博不能至其约。《聂会东文集》不但对我们研究医学发展史有所裨益，重要的是文集中充溢着的仁心仁术更是晚辈后学所应汲取的精神财富。

在“逝者如斯”的时光长河中，人们总想抓住某些永恒的东西。春秋时鲁国大夫叔孙豹喻“立德”“立功”“立言”为“三不朽”。“立德”，即树立道德；“立功”，即为国为民建立功绩；“立言”，即提出具有真知灼见的言论。此三者成为许多仁人志士孜孜以求的永恒价值。

聂会东在华40年行医、建院、办学，籍高尚的医德、精湛的医术、渊博的学识，在中国现代医学发展的进程中“立德”“立功”“立言”，造福广大民众，他的历史功绩当为后人铭记。

本书付梓之际，拉杂数言，简属弁端，供海内外关心、关注、支持齐鲁医学发展的各界朋友参考，是为序。

山东大学齐鲁医院党委书记　曹宪忠

2018年12月

序二

中国的现代医学肇始于西方教会在中国的籍医传教。

1807 年 9 月 7 日，英国伦敦会传教士罗伯特·马礼逊(Robert Marrison，1782～1834)抵达广州，揭开了近代基督教新教在华传教的历史，同时也启动了以医疗活动为手段，以传播基督福音为目的的“藉医传教”的历程。

1860 年，第二次鸦片战争结束。随着一系列不平等条约的签订，西方教会进一步扩大了他们在中国的传教范围，教会医疗事业也随之进入新的发展时期。19 世纪六七十年代，教会医疗事业在沿海、沿江地区拓展的同时，开始向内地渗透。山东的现代医学亦即发轫于此时期。

论及山东现代医学的源起和发展，有一个人是绕不开去的，他在山东现代医学史上是一位承上启下的重要人物，他就是聂会东。

聂会东(英文名 James Boyd Neal)，美北长老会医学传教士，1855 年出生，1883 年来到中国，1922 年因病回到美国，1925 年逝世。他曾担任中华博医会会长、齐鲁大学医学院院长、齐鲁大学校长，是济南华美医院(齐鲁医院前身)、华美医校、美国登州长老会医院、济南基督教共合医道学堂、齐鲁大学医科的创始人和主要创办者。他是受人尊重、技术高超的医生，更是山东现代医学教育事业的开创者，为山东乃至全国现代医学事业的发展做出了重要贡献。

就是这样一位在山东现代医学发展史上举足轻重的人物，由于历史的原因我们手头掌握的与他相关的史料却少得可怜，甚至直到 2014 年我们还没有他的一张正面照片。要感谢我们的校友、美国密歇根大学的亓念宁教授和他的夫人。2014 年，亓教授受邀到山东大学做学术交流和访问，带来了他翻拍的一张背面有聂会东留言和签名的照片，这也是迄今为止我们所看到的唯一一张聂会东先生的正面像。此外，他回到美国后又通过电子邮件发来了由他的夫人挖掘整理的介绍聂会东生平的资料，虽然相对简单，但却首次丰富了我们对聂会东的认识。

2015～2016 年，本书的主译者之一，山东大学齐鲁医院护理部的曹英娟同志受国家留学基金委委派赴美国约翰·霍普金斯大学访问交流。其间，她在霍普金斯大学图书馆、耶鲁大学图书馆、费城美国长老会总部图书馆、澳大利亚国立图书馆，发现并收集整理了大量有关西方教会组织在山东开创和发展现代医学视野的文字资料和图片，其中一部分涉及聂会东本人，这对我们全面了解聂会东提供了很大帮助。

2017 年适逢齐鲁大学成立 100 周年，源自于齐鲁大学医科的"齐鲁医学"也整整走过了 100 个年头。为了缅怀先贤，铭记历史，继承和弘扬"齐鲁医学"100 年来积淀形成的文化品格和精神内涵，山东大学举办了一系列纪念活动。聂会东作为山东现代医学事业、齐鲁大学医科和"齐鲁医学"品牌的主要创立者，理应为"齐鲁医学"品牌的传承者们所铭记。为此，我们感到有责任将所掌握的聂会东的英文史料译介给大家，遂决定翻译出版这本《聂会东文集》。此举得到了山东大学党委和领导的充分肯定和大力支持！在本书的编译出版过程中，山东大学原党委常务副书记李建军同志百忙中多次过问本书的编译出版情况并作出指示，给了我们莫大的关怀和鼓励，在此表示衷心的感谢！

《聂会东文集》共收录 1888～1939 年的 25 篇文稿，凡 10 万余字。其中聂氏的学术文章、工作报告、书信 20 篇，聂会东夫人文稿 2 篇，其余 3 篇为友人纪念聂会东及夫人的文稿。本书的翻译团队是由齐鲁医院一群朝气蓬勃的年轻博士、硕士组成的，他们中大多数有海外求学经历，有很好的英文功底和对此项工作极高的热情，又加之均具医学背景，故绝大多数文稿翻译起来都得心应手。困难的是，中国的人名、地名、官职名和其他专用名词以及外国人的名字由西文回译到中文，有时要花费很多的时间和精力去翻阅文献加以考证。虽然做起来很苦、很累，但“累并快乐着”。感谢他们的辛勤努力和付出！

他们虽然竭尽全力，但译文中不妥甚或错误之处恐在所难免，深望海内外专家和读者朋友不吝赐教。期望该书能为中国现代医学史的研究提供借鉴和参考。

山东大学齐鲁医院院长　李新钢

2018年12月

目录

纪念聂会东夫妇

文 集

信　件

附　录

齐鲁医院创始人之一美北长老会传教士聂会东(James Boyd Neal)博士

1911 年 4 月 17 日，山东巡抚孙宝琦（前排中间者）出席共合医道学堂（现新兴楼）落成典礼（第二排中间侧身者为聂会东）

1911 年共合医道学堂学生与教职人员在新兴楼前合影（后排左三为聂会东）

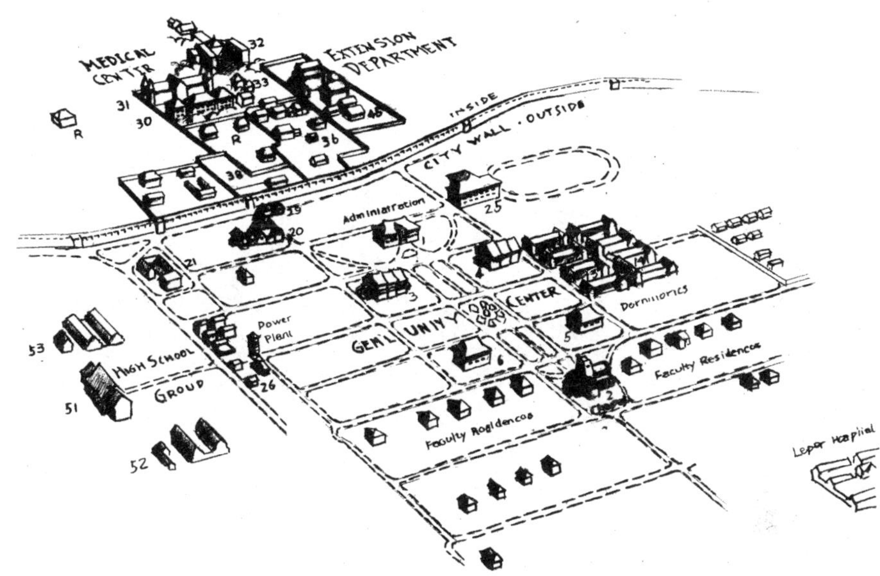

齐鲁大学及附属医院鸟瞰图

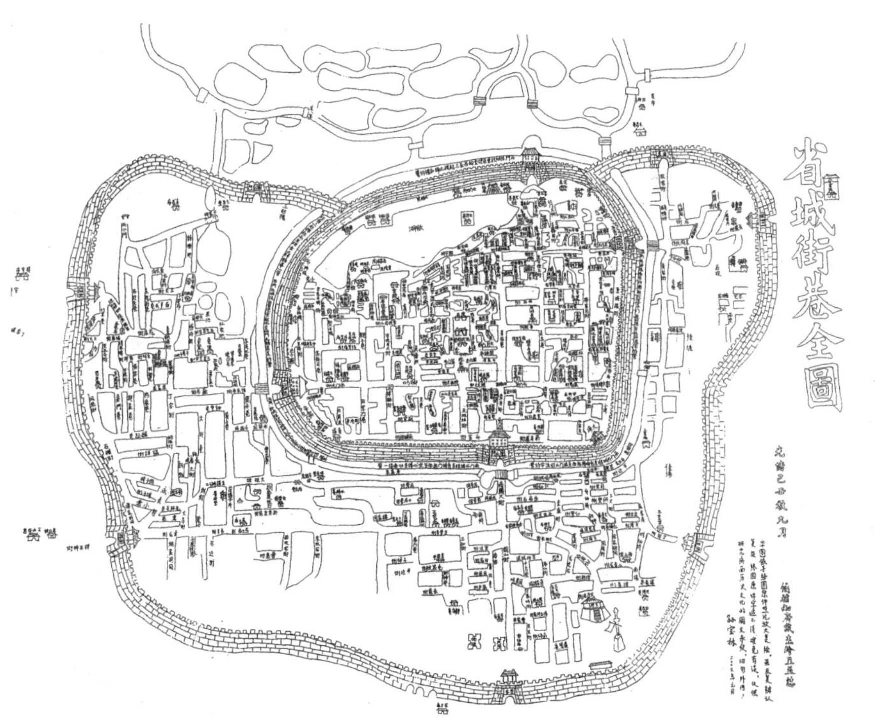

1889 年(光绪十五年)济南市街巷地图

1935 年建成的博施楼(现山东大学齐鲁医院科研楼)下东南角奠基石上面“博施济众”四字为时任国民政府卫生部部长刘瑞恒所书

建于 1904 年的被历史学家翦伯赞誉为“中国博览馆建筑的代表”的广智院

齐鲁大学女生宿舍景兰斋

齐鲁大学男生宿舍 400 号院

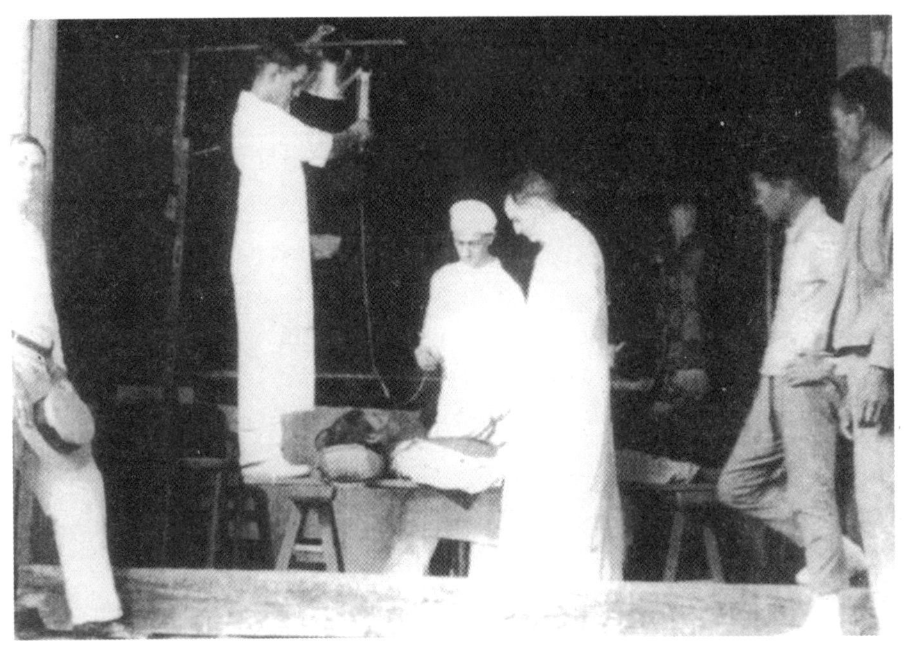

1919年,鲁中地区发生严重的霍乱疫情,齐鲁医院组建医疗队深入疫区诊治。这是医疗队在一个佛教寺庙里设立的临时诊疗点

医疗下乡巡诊

纪念聂会东夫妇

纪念聂会东医生

1925 年 2 月 4 日，聂会东医生(Dr. Jame Boyd Neal)在宾夕法尼亚州的费城去世，他自 1922 年因病退休后就一直居住在此。

聂会东于 1855 生于宾夕法尼亚，1877 年毕业于耶鲁大学(Yale University)。随后，他在谢菲尔德科技学院医学预科学习两年后进入宾夕法尼亚大学(University of Pennsylvania)的医学院学习医学，并于 1883 年毕业，同年携夫人前往中国。

到中国后，聂会东夫妇住在狄考文博士在登州(Tengchow)的家中，在那里学习汉语。聂会东的汉语水平，体现在他在中国期间翻译的多本书籍。结合他在登州医院和药房的工作，他开始教授医学生。1890 年，他被调到济南，那里的医疗工作已由洪士提凡医生(Dr. Stephen Hunter)开创。济南中心街道上的一个小房间是唯一作为药房的地方。后来在东郊购置一块土地，以建文璧医院。聂会东第一次从美国休假回来时，文璧医院(McIlvaine Hospital)基础工程的建设工作已经完成。在接下来的一年，聂会东完成了病房和医科学生教室的建设。

聂会东与来自沂州府(Ichowfu)的章嘉礼医生(Dr. Johnson)以及来自青州府(Tsing-chowfu)和邹平(Chouping)的英国浸礼会(English Baptist Mission)的医生合作开展“巡回医学教育”，这是齐鲁大学医学院的发端，后来成为基督教大学(Christian University)的一部分，聂医生曾长期担任医学院院长。

聂会东的优秀品质和专业能力引起了省外同道的关注。因此，他于 1903 年被选为中国博医会(China Medical Missionary Association)的主席。虽然他只担任这一职位三年，但他在博医会的影响力却一直存在。1919 年，他被选为山东基督教大学(Shantung Christian University)校长，担任这一职务，直到 1921 年 1 月，他突发重病，迫使他停下了所有的工作。1922 年，他回到美国，居住在费城直到去世。

在中国期间，他把极大的热情和精力投入医学著作和医学名词的译介中，并取得了很大成绩，《化学辨质》《眼科证治》和《皮科证治》就是他的代表译著。他是中国博医会医学术语委员会的负责人之一。作为一个老师，他主要教授眼科学和生物化学。

聂医生深受他的同事们喜爱。他是个忠实的朋友，慷慨、热情、富有同情心。他平等地对待同事、学生和大众，他非常礼貌、体贴、细心、乐于助人。尽管他自己没有孩子，但是他很喜欢孩子，许多传教士的孩子和中国当地老百姓的孩子经常在他家里一待就是几个月，他对他们视如己出，像父亲般地呵护、照顾他们。相信这些孩子长大后，在内心深处会对先生充满感恩之情。

我们对聂夫人深表同情，她是他忠诚的妻子和助手。聂会东先生的去世，使夫人的内心承受了巨大的痛苦和孤独，在今后的生活中她将面临种种艰难困苦和考验。

（摘自 *American Preseyterian Shantung Mission*，1925）

In Memoriam: Dr. James Boyd Neal

On February 4th. 1925, Dr. James Boyd Neal died in Philadelphia, Pa. , where he had been living since his retirement from the field, on account of illness, in 1922.

Dr. Neal was born in Pennsylvania in 1855 and was graduated from the Yale University in 1877. Following this he took a two-year course at the Sheffield Scientific School preparatory to the study of medicine. He entered the School of Medicine of the University of Pennsylvania, and was graduated there from in 1883, coming to China the same year with Mrs. Neal.

Dr. and Mrs. Neal lived first at Tengchow in the home of Dr. Calvin Mateer, where they studied the Chinese language. Dr. Neal's proficiency in it may be judged by the number of medical books he translated during his years in China. In connection with the hospital and dispensary work in which he was engaged in Tengchow, he began the teaching of classes of students in medicine. In 1890 he was transferred to Tsinan where medical work had been begun by Dr. Stephen Hunter. A small room on the main street was the only place that could be obtained for a dispensary. Later a plot of land was obtained in the East suburb, and on his return from his first furlough, the McIlvaine Hospital was ready. In the following year Dr. Neal completed the building of the wards for in-patients and a separate court for his medical students.

Dr. Neal conducted the so-called "peripatetic" medical school in co-operation with Dr. Johnson, of Ichowfu, and with physicians of the English-Baptist Mission at Tsing-chowfu and Chouping. This was the beginning of the Medical College, which became one of the units of the Christian University, and Dr. Neal was its Dean for many years.

Dr. Neal's fine qualities and ability early attracted attention outside of Shantung, and in 1903 he was elected President of the China Medical Missionary Association, a position in which he served for three years, and was thereafter always influential in its councils. In 1919 he was elected President of the Shantung Christian University, and served as such until January 1921, when a sudden illness laid him permanently aside from all active work. He returned to America in 1922, and lived at Philadelphia up to the time of his death.

During all the years he was on the field, he was greatly interested in the building up of medical literature in Chinese and was translator of books on Physiological Chemistry, Ophthalmology, and Dermatology. He was one of the leaders in forming the Committee on Scientific Terminology for China. As a teacher, his name was especially associated with Ophthalmology and Physiological Chemistry.

Dr. Neal was greatly beloved by all his associates. He was a loyal friend, generous, warm-hearted and sympathetic. In all his relationships with colleagues, students, and the general public he was courteous, considerate and helpful. Although never blest with children of his own, he was devotedly fond of children, and was foster-father to many missionary children who spent months in his home, and they, together with many Chinese children, will rise up and call him blessed.

Our hearts go out in deep sympathy to Mrs. Neal, his devoted wife and helper, in this her great trial and loneliness.

一位传教士眼中的聂会东

William Hamilton Jefferys

我们的传道会(中国博医会,The China Medical Missionary Society)主席聂会东博士,1855 年出生于宾夕法尼亚州东部,1877 年毕业于耶鲁大学。其后他在纽黑文市的科技学校学习了两年的医学预科课程,并为了得到商业经验在一家银行实习了一个冬天。在这以后他进入宾夕法尼亚大学医学院学习并于 1883 年毕业。他是这所全美国高校中最有代表性的大学的毕业生,它的医学院历史最为悠久并且在美国医学院校中享有盛名。他跻身于那些才智非凡且技术过硬的人的行列,成为从事医学传教工作的上佳人选。

也是在 1883 年,聂会东博士及夫人来到中国并居住在登州——一座靠近芝罘(Chefoo)的城市;1890 年,他们接受教会派遣到济南府(Chinanfu),并一直在此工作。在此期间,他们回国两次并在山东的另一个传教站代职一年,所以他整个职业生涯都是在山东度过的。他在我们中间知名度很高,他与生俱来的幽默风趣,令人印象深刻。

除了在治病救人方面有过硬的本领和技术外,聂会东博士还对医学教育有着浓厚的兴趣,为此付出了他人所不能及的辛劳和努力,成功地培养了医学生,取得了巨大的成绩,这也是他之所以被我们铭记在心的原因。多年以前,我曾在费城听到他的演讲,我清晰地记得他对从事医学教育严谨的态度、执着的信念、丰富的设想。到目前为止,他已经教授了 4 个医科班的学生,其中 2 个班的教学工作是由在山东的其他医生的协助下完成的。他培养的 20 多个医学生中,绝大部分非常出色地完成了学业。按照原来的计划,聂会东博士目前正致力于和山东的英国浸礼会一起联合开展教育工作,计划的一部分是联合组建一所医学院校,这所院校将比在山东省创建的其他院校的教学效果更好。

其实，我们在这里谈论主席的性格或为人是完全没有必要的，因为我们中间大多数人对他是非常了解的，无论是作为一名医生还是一位绅士。更何况，在背后评价和议论某个人是不礼貌的，也是令人不愉快的，且容易引起别人的反感——无论这种议论或评价是有意还是无意的。我还记得在那次费城之行中发生的一件事，那件事让我笃信聂会东博士是一位谦谦君子，他天生不喜欢炫耀。他给我们展示了一面锦旗，上面写着赞美之情的话语。中国人习惯于用这种方式表达个人的欣赏、尊重和其他美好的情感。这个锦旗可以说是华丽的，上面绣着金字，又大又美观，备受赞赏，引起了我们极大的兴趣。大家问了许多问题并要求翻译锦旗上文字的内容。谦虚的博士极力向大家说明翻译的困难，但大家仍能够感觉到文字所表达的对他的赞美和感谢。我不会忘记这一天，可爱又可怜的聂会东博士试图模糊旗子上那些溢美之词的意思，以求让他的美国朋友认为那些华丽辞藻无任何意义。

所以我们不应该再对聂医生品头论足，让我们团结起来，以我们的主席为荣，并为我们能将自己的福祉寄托在这样一个有才华的公仆身上而感到由衷的欣慰和喜悦。让我们与他携手共进，为实现他所制定的任何有利于未来发展的切实可行的宏伟蓝图奉献自己的智慧和汗水。

[摘自 *The China Medical Missionary Journal*, 1903, 17(1)]

James Boyd Neal, M.D.

Dr. James Boyd Neal, President of the Society, was born in Eastern Pennsylvania in the year 1855 and educated at Yale, graduating in 1877. This was followed by a two-year course in the scientific school in New Haven, preparatory to the study of medicine, and this in turn by a winter spent in a bank to get a little business experience. He then entered the medical school of the University of Pennsylvania and graduated there from in 1883. He is thus a graduate of the most representative of all American colleges and of the oldest and deservedly best known of American schools of medicine, and stands among the ranks of those who hold that no form of intellectual and professional training is too thorough to be best suited to medical missionary work.

In that same year, 1883, Dr. and Mrs. Neal came to China and settled in Teng-chou, near Chefoo, until 1890, when they were transferred to Chi nanfu. In this place they have worked ever since, with the exception of the time consumed in two trips home and a year of substituting in another station in Shantung. So his whole professional life has been spent in this one province, in which it is well known among us that he is very naturally greatly interested and with which he is thoroughly identified.

As have most other men of ability, Dr. Neal has a hobby, a part of his work in which he has invested more of his big heart than any other, and that is saying a great deal when we remember the heart and the work of which we are speaking. I am referring to his devoted interest and success in the training of medical students. Years ago, it seems to me, I heard him speak on the subject in Philadelphia, and I easily remember the earnestness of his address on this subject and the seeming soundness of his ideas. So far four classes have passed through his hands, in two of which he was assisted by other physicians in Shantung, and twenty odd men have been trained by him, the majority of whom have done very creditably. In pursuance of the old interest, Dr. Neal's attention is centered at present in a proposed union with the English Baptist Mission of Shantung in educational work, one part of the scheme being to unite in a medical school, which will be far more efficient than anything so far established in that province.

It would be superfluous to write to his fellows in China of the personal characteristics of our President. He is well known to most of us as physician and man. Besides all this, personalities are not usually pleasant, whether intended to be so or not so intended, and from an incident that I also remember in connection with that same visit to Philadelphia, I am led to believe that Dr. Neal is one of those genuinely modest men who by nature are averse to personalities. He was showing us a specimen of those complimentary effusions, by means of which the Chinese are accustomed to express appreciation, regard and other sentiments in a personal and, to say the least, very flowery fashion. The particular effusion in question was in the shape of a flag inscribed in gold characters and was large and handsome. It was much admired, and inspired great interest. Many questions were asked, and finally a translation called for. The poor Doctor plead difficulty of rendering the character, etc., but it was of no avail and I have not forgotten to this day the delightful wretchedness of Dr. Neal when trying to slur over those honeyed phrases and impress upon an American audience that nothing meant anything, and everything meant nothing.

So we shall not go into personalities with the Doctor a second time, but let us rather collectively as a Society take pride in our President and heartily congratulate ourselves that its welfare is entrusted to so capable a servant, and let us give him our co-operation and allegiance in whatever plans he may make for further growth and usefulness.

纪念聂会东夫人

聂会东夫人于1939年8月4日在宾夕法尼亚州匹兹堡逝世。她被公认为长老会山东差会中最能干、最有能力的传教士之一，也是一名可以信赖的朋友。

她于1883年和丈夫聂会东医生一起来到登州(Tengchow)，从事传教工作。1890年，他们来到济南(Tsinan)。她没有自己的孩子，但她却常常照顾教会中其他传教士的孩子，以使他们的母亲毫无后顾之忧地在乡村巡回传教。有时候她自己也去济南近郊的村子里传教，并且在那里创办女子短期学习班，是一名深受当地妇女爱戴的好老师。

她与生俱来就具有老师的天赋和特质。她做到了诲人不倦。有时候她也到她丈夫工作的位于济南东郊的医院进行传教。她总是以极大的热情和精力讲授《旧约圣经》的故事和基督教义。这深深吸引了患者，他们常常把病床移到她的周围靠近她，不想错过她说的每一句话。此外，她也在男子学校教授算术。

同时，她还是一名出色的管理者。除了把家庭打理得井井有条之外，每逢男子学校校长韩维廉(Hamilton)先生外出巡回传教时，也总是由她来负责管理学校。彼时教会在芝罘(Chefoo)为新来的传教士开办了一所语言学校，为了办好这所学校，她远离自己的丈夫，在学校里她既是是管理者，也亲自授课，为此做出了巨大牺牲。

她善于与人交往，与她相处总有一种如沐春风的感觉。在济南府，凡是与她交往过的人，无论是中国的高级官员还是其他外籍人士，都认为她是一位非常有魅力的贤内助。她做医生的丈夫创立了现在的齐鲁医学院，并曾于1919年担任齐鲁大学(Cheeloo University)的校长。

她谦虚、低调，不事张扬，以至于她做的很多工作都不为人所知。

她很坚强，在中国的40年，尽管身体上遭受了很多的痛苦，但她总是积极快乐地面对工作和生活。

最重要的是，她是一个有思想、值得信赖的朋友，深受与她一起工作的所有传教士的喜爱。

（摘自 *American Presbyterian Church Minute of The Shantung Mission*，1940）

In Memoriam: Mrs. James Boyd Neal

The death of Mrs. James Boyd Neal occurred on August 4, 1939 at Pittsburgh, Pennsylvania. She is remembered as one of the most efficient, capable missionaries the Shantung Mission has had and as a faithful friend.

Her service began in 1883, when, with her husband, Doctor Neal, she came to Tengchow. In 1890 they were moved to Tsinan. Having no children of her own, she was constantly seeking out her family in Christ. Sometimes she mothered the children of other missionaries, permitting their own mothers to itinerate in country villages. Sometimes she herself went into the villages and was a fine teacher of country women in short term classes held in Tsinan.

She was a born teacher, loving to impart information to others. Sometimes she was found teaching daily in the hospital in the East Suburb, Tsinan, where her husband was at work. Many times the beds were moved so the patients might be near her, as she taught the Old Testament stories and doctrines with great earnestness and power. Again she was found teaching arithmetic in the Boys' school.

She was also an executive. Her home was noted for the efficiency with which it was managed. When Mr. Hamilton, Principal of the Boys' school, was itinerating, she was left in charge. When a language school was opened for new missionaries one year in Chefoo, she left her husband's side, a great sacrifice for her and managed that school and was able herself to act as one of the teachers.

She was social in her nature, loving to entertain. High Chinese officials, and people of many nationalities in that provincial capital of Tsinan, found a charming hostess in the wife of the doctor who began what is now Cheeloo medical school, and who acted as President of the Cheeloo University in 1919.

She was modest about her own service and many did not know of her varied activities in preaching the Gospel.

She was courageous. She suffered from bodily discomfort all her forty years in China, yet was active and cheerful all her days.

Most of all, she was a thoughtful, faithful friend, beloved by all the missionaries with whom she worked.

文　集

回归热

聂会东 著

1880 年冬、春两季，在中国山东的多个地区发生了罕见的食物短缺，有些地区实际上演变成了饥荒，而在其他地区，就像笔者之前的传教站登州府一样，则仅是导致了日常主食的价格疯涨。

6 月初，我从疫情才刚开始流行的饥荒地区返回了登州，发现在过去几个月中登州发生了不同寻常的流行性发热疫情。目前在医院治疗的发热患者约 22 例，其中 10 例诊断为回归热。从这 10 个病例中，我选择了 6 例进行报告，一方面是因为他们的体温统计表十分明确地显示出周期性发热的典型表现（唯一例外的是 3 号病例）；另一方面是因为患者的其他症状与多种诊断对该病的描述几乎一致，所以诊断上没有疑问。

通过对后面病例记录的研究可以发现，在这些病例中几乎总是会出现并可以被认为具有诊断意义的症状包括以下几项：恶心和胆汁性呕吐；或轻或重的黄疸，表现为皮肤及小便发黄；肌肉和关节严重疼痛，给患者带来巨大痛苦；出现症状复发。

第一轮发热一般持续 3～5 天，第一轮间歇期则持续 5～10 天。第二轮发热也持续 3～5 天。在还会出现第三轮发热的患者中，第二轮间歇期会持续很短，只有 1 天。同时第三次发热也相应地很短暂，仅在一个患者超过了 2 天。在所有病例中我都没有观察到出现超过 2 次热回归（也即共出现 3 次单独、明显的发热过程）的患者。正如所观察到的，复发的发热通常比第一次发热温度要高，无论是第一次或第二次发热，都会在转折点骤降。所记录到的最高发热体温达到 107.2 ℉和 108 ℉，常见的发热体温范围是103 ℉到 105 ℉，这些非常高的体温只出现在转折点时（即体温骤降前）。该病有时还可罕见地伴有精神症状。所有病例中均未见伤寒症状。该病的康复期总是很长，病人因发热而感到体力显著下降，需要很长时间才能恢复到以前的健康状态。间歇期的特点是除乏力、偶有轻微疼痛及黄疸外没有其他任何症状。该病似乎没有非常强的传染性，7 个与患者密切接触的人中仅有一个患病。在我的病例中，治疗方法多数是简单地给予牛奶和稀粥规律饮食，当体温超过 103.5 ℉时给予安替比林、乙酰苯胺等药物治疗。

病例记录：

病例一，男，21 岁，大学学者。

体质并不强壮。进行体温测量前两天已经发病，症状包括头痛、恶心及发热，发病第二天偶尔出现畏寒。在发病后前 3 天内，呕吐多次，呕吐物为食物、胆汁和蛔虫。腹痛明显但无腹部压痛，双腿疼痛，黄疸。首次发热持续 6 天，体温骤然下降，间歇期持续 8 天；第二次发热持续 5 天。有一晚出现神志不清。

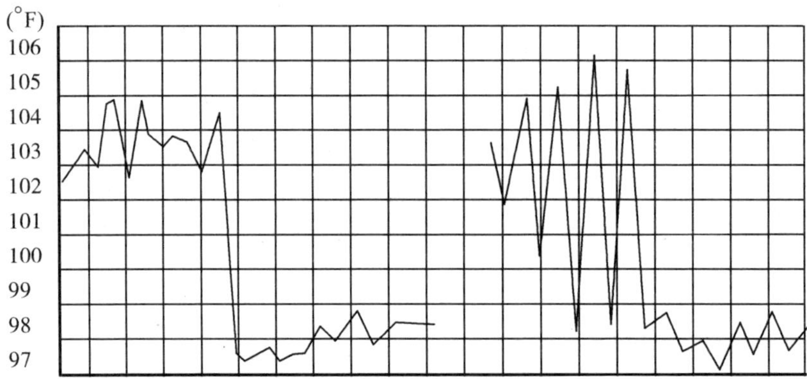

病例二：男，农民。

身体素质良好。发热第二天入院，体温 105 ℉，无恶心或呕吐症状。之后双腿疼痛明显，多次呕吐，黄疸。第一次发热持续 5 天，间歇期 1 天；第二次发热 3 天，间歇期 1 天；第三次发热持续 1 天。

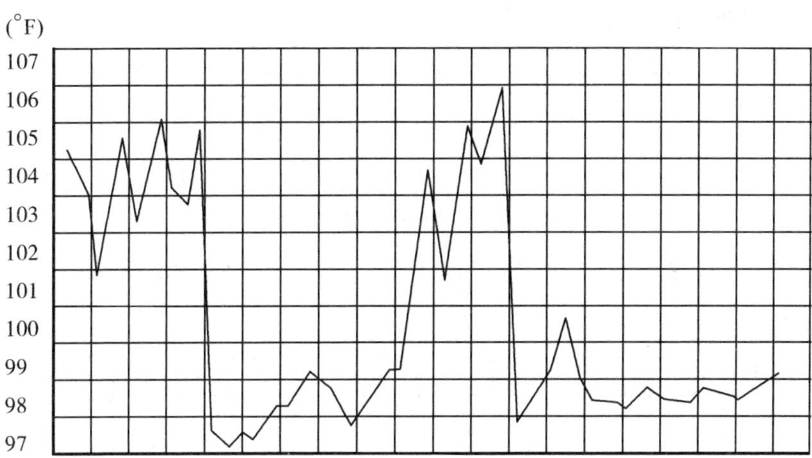

病例三:男,33 岁,医学生。

身体平时非常强壮。发病时感觉发热、头痛、头晕,后出现恶心及呕吐酸性液体,皮肤发黄,尿液呈深色(呕吐物和尿液中显示出含有胆汁、胃酸还有糖),并出现双腿肌肉及手指关节剧烈和持续的疼痛。经过 12 天的持续高烧,他的体温逐渐下降到正常,期间未出现精神症状或任何伤寒症状,但他的恢复非常缓慢。没有复发。我之所以把这一病例与其他更典型的回归热病例放在一起,是因为该例的综合症状比较明显地提示其诊断就是回归热而不是其他发热性疾病。尽管我也清楚该例病人的诊断仍有可质疑的地方,尤其是第五天患者腹部出现了轻微的散在性皮疹(表现为稍突起的暗红色斑点),虽然此患者没有出现伤寒症状,但这仍提示了斑疹伤寒的可能性。

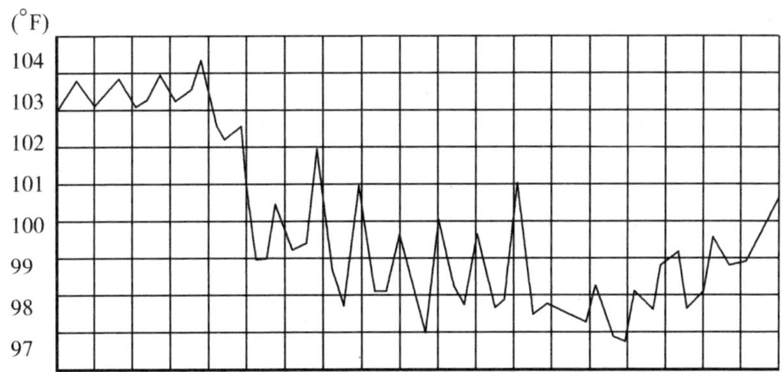

病例四：男，19 岁，乞丐。

营养不良，身体虚弱。前期症状表现为头痛、畏寒、全身疼痛，后出现呕吐，严重黄疸，手臂、双腿、及指关节疼痛。发热持续 3 天后突然退热，发热间歇期 10 天，第二次发热持续了 2 天，症状与之前大致一样，但疼痛部位更明显地集中于大关节，如双肩。有意思的是本例患者发热间歇期很长。他在发热停止 8 天后被送回家，这也是他的体温监测中断的原因。

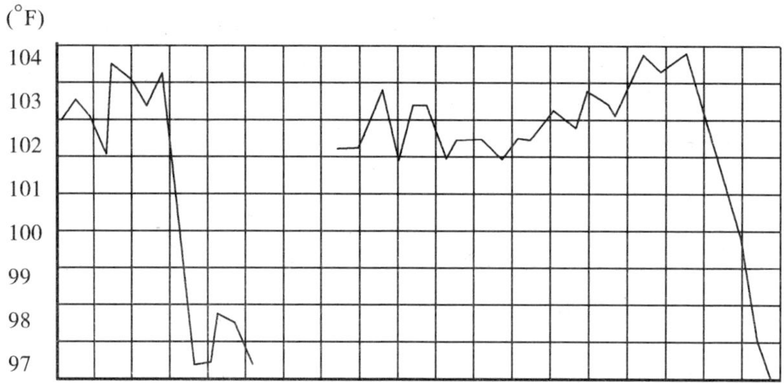

病例五：男，22 岁，农民。

发热症状出现的第四天入院，初期症状是疼痛、恶心和呕吐。黄疸较重，尿液颜色深。在 6 天的间歇期之后又再次发热，同时伴有腹泻和呕吐，无四肢疼痛。发热 5 天之后又再次退烧了，间歇期 1 天，再次发热了 7 天，此时他自行离开了医院。偶有轻微的精神错乱症状。

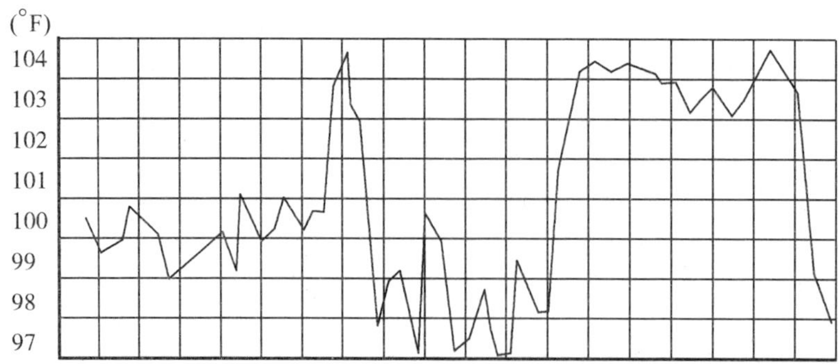

病例六：男，21 岁，家仆。

营养良好。初期症状全身不适及疼痛，第二天出现膝关节及肩关节剧烈疼痛。轻微黄疸、恶心，第一次发热持续了 6 天，在间歇期的前 4 天他仍诉大关节疼痛。经过 6 天的间歇期，再次发热并持续 4 天，在降温前的转折点，最高体温达到了 108 ℉，随后体温骤然下降，并降至正常体温以下，但低体温仅持续了一天，随后体温再次升高至 101.5 ℉，后降至正常。

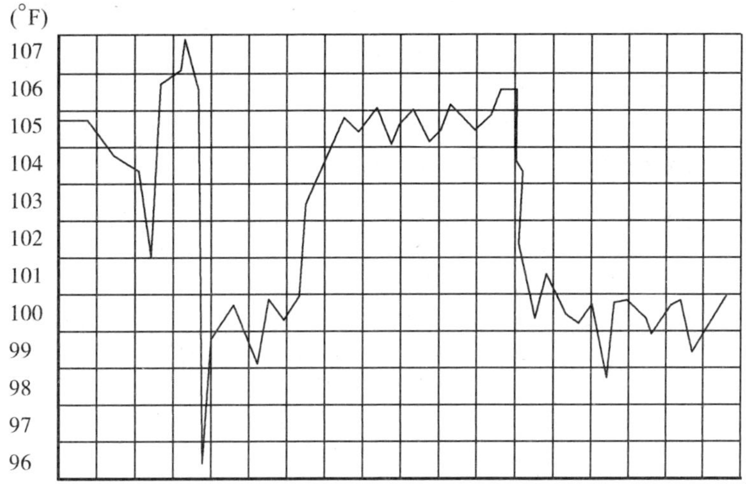

［摘自 *China Medical Missionary Journal*, 1889, 4(4)］

Relapsing or Famine Fever

By James Boyd Neal, M. D.

During the winter and spring of 1880, unusual scarcity prevailed in many parts of the province of Shantung, China, amounting in some parts to actual famine, in others, as in the writer's former prefecture of Tungchow-fu, to merely very high prices for the ordinary staples of food.

Returning early in June from the famine region, where reports of fever were just beginning to prevail, I found during the causing few months an unusual prevalence of fever in Tungchowfu, there being some twenty-two cases under treatment in hospital, ten of which were diagnosed as Relapsing Fever. From these ten cases, I have selected six for reporting upon, partly because their temperature charts show so plainly the attacks and remissions of fever, the only exception being that of No. 3, and partly because the other symptoms correspond so nearly to the descriptions of the disease given by various authors as to leave no room for doubt as to the diagnosis.

As will be seen by an examination of the appended notes, the symptoms which were almost invariably present in these cases, and which may be considered diagnostic of the disease, were nausea and bilious vomiting; jaundice, slight or severe, shown not only in the yellowness of the surface but also by the presence of bile in the urine; pains in the muscles and joints, usually severe and causing the patient much distress; and finally the occurrence of relapses.

The duration of the first attack of fever ranged from three to five days, the first intermission from five to ten days, the second attack of fever from three to five days, the second intermission, in cases where there was a third attack, being very short, only one day, while the third attack was also correspondingly short, only in one case exceeding two days. In no case did I observe more than two relapses, that is, three separate and distinct attacks of fever. As will be observed, the fever in the relapse usually ran higher than in the first attack, and always, whether in the first or second attack, fell by crisis. The highest temperatures reached were 107.2 ℉ and 108 ℉, the usual range being from 103 ℉ to 105 ℉, these very high temperatures showing themselves only at the time of a crisis. Delirium was a very infrequent accompaniment of the disease, while low typhoid symptoms were not observed in a single case. The convalescence was always much protracted, the patient finding his strength very much reduced by the fever, and requiring a long time to get back to his former state of health. The intermissions were characterized by no symptoms except loss of strength and occasionally a slight persistence of the pains and jaundice. It did not seem to be virulently contagious. Only one of seven people, who were in intimate contact with the patients, took the disease. Treatment in my cases consisted for the most part simply of milk and gruel diet at regular intervals, with antipyrin or antifebrin when the temperature rose above 103.5 ℉.

Record of Casks.

Case No. 1.—Male, age 21, scholar in college.

Is not naturally strong. Disease began two days before temperature observations were taken, with headache, nausea and fever, second day felt chilly at times. Vomited a number of times during first three days, ejecta consisting of food, bile and round worms. Complained of a good deal of pain in stomach but no tenderness on pressure, and of pains in his legs; jaundiced. First attack of fever six days. Temperature fell by crisis, and intermission lasted eight days, second fever five days. Was delirious one night.

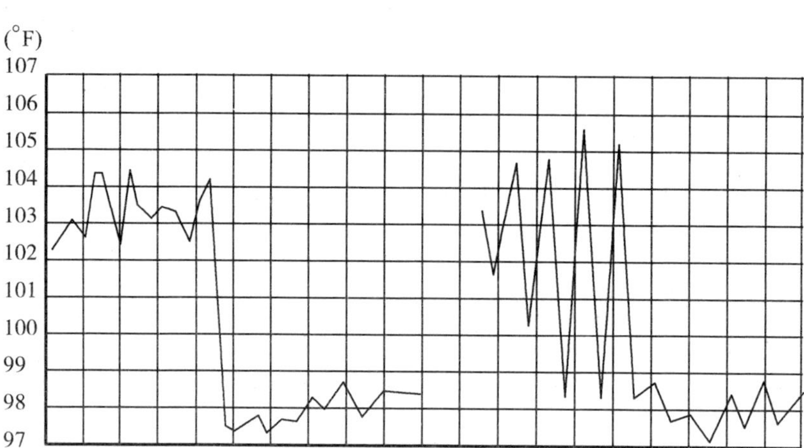

Case No. 2.—Male, farmer.

Good physique. Came in on second day of fever with temperature of 105 ℉, giving no history of nausea or vomiting. Complained afterwards of pains in legs, pretty sever, and vomited several times, sonic jaundice. First fever five days, intermission one days, second fever three days, intermission one day, third fever one day.

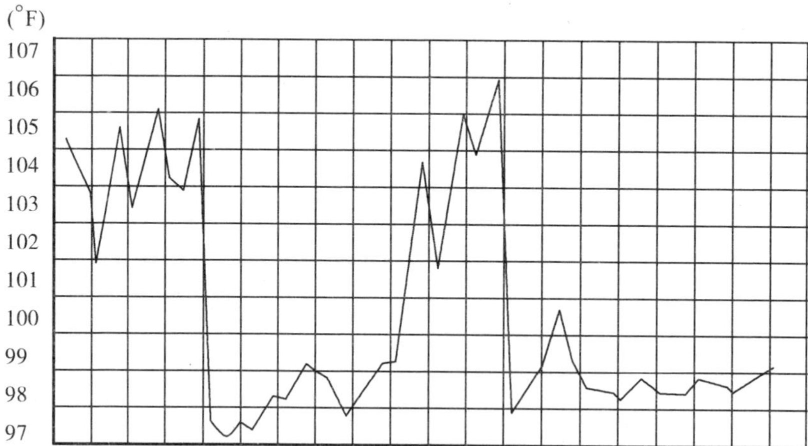

Case No. 3.—Male, age 33, medical student.

Usually very strong and robust. Disease began with feeling of feverishness, headache and dizziness, succeeded by nausea and vomiting up of sour liquid, yellowness of surface and dark colored urine, showing presence of bile on addition of sulphuric acid and sugar, and by severe and constant pains in muscles of legs and joints of fingers. After twelve days of continued fever, without delirium or any low typhoid symptoms, his temperature gradually declined to normal, but his convalescence was very slow. He had no relapse. I have included this case among the more undoubted cases of Relapsing Fever because I think the general ensemble of symptoms point more clearly to its being this disease than any other fever, although I am aware there is room for doubt, especially as a slight discrete rash of slightly raised dark red spots declared itself about the fifth day on his abdomen and arras, pointing to the possibility of its being Typhus, though no typhoid symptoms were developed.

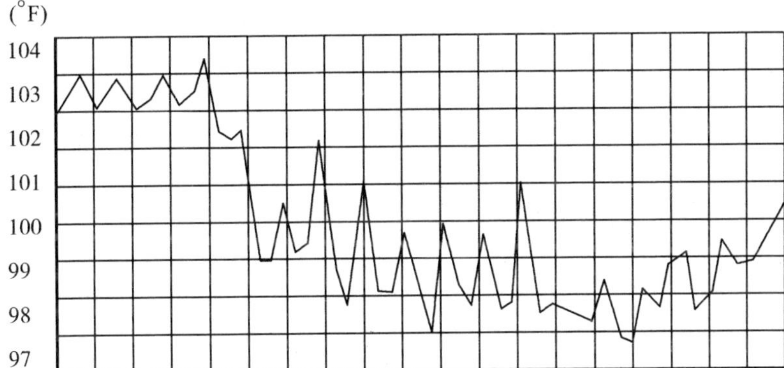

Case No. 4.—Male, ago 19, beggar.

Underfed, weakly. Disease began with headache, chilliness, general pains, followed by vomiting, severe jaundice, and pains in arms and legs and knuckles. He had fever for only three days, when it suddenly left him and he was free from fever for ten days, when he had another attack, which lasted for only two days, the symptoms being about the same, the pains, however, being more distinctly localized in the larger joints, such as his shoulders, elbows and lips. His case is interesting as showing a very long interval between the attacks. He had been sent home after eight days' freedom from fever, which explains the hiatus in the observations of temperature.

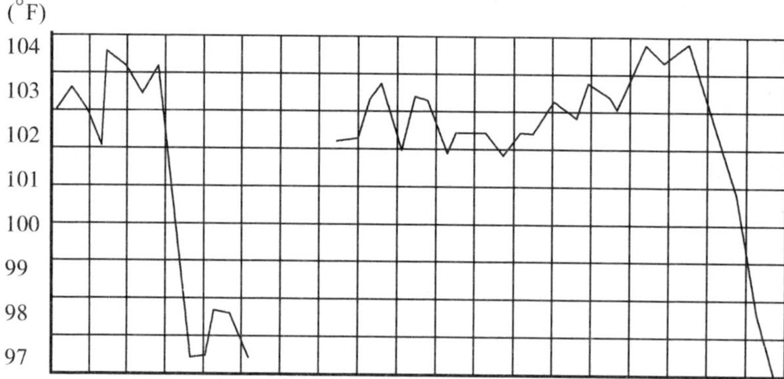

Case No. 5.—Male, age 22, farmer.

Came in on fourth day of fever. Began with general pain nausea and vomiting. Heavily jaundiced; urine dark colored. During the relapse, which came on after six days intermission, he suffered from diarrhoea and vomiting. Complained very little or none at all of pains in limbs. Fever left him the second time after five day; but he was granted only one day's respite, it set in again and continued seven days, when he ran away. Was slightly delirious at times.

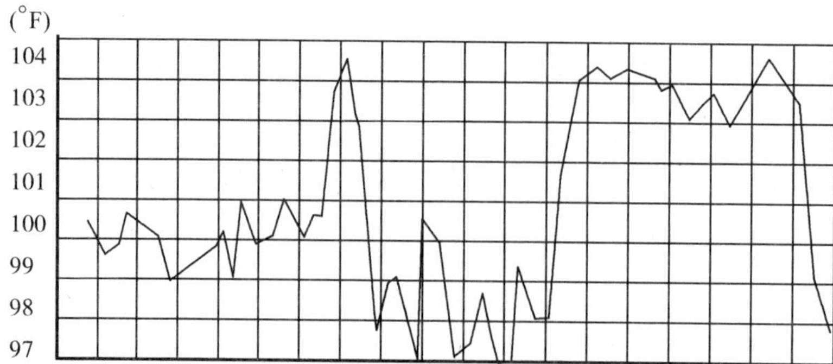

Case No. 6.—Male, age 21, house servant.

Well-nourished. Began with malaise and general pains, followed on second day by severe pains in knee and shoulder joints. Slightly jaundiced and nauseated, first attack of fever lasted six days, and during the first four days of the intermission he still complained some of pains in large joints. After six days' freedom from fever he had a second attack of four days, during which, at the time of the crisis, his temperature reached 108 ℉. It fell immediately, however, to below normal, but continued low for one day, rising afterwards to only 101.5 ℉ for the day and then declining to the normal.

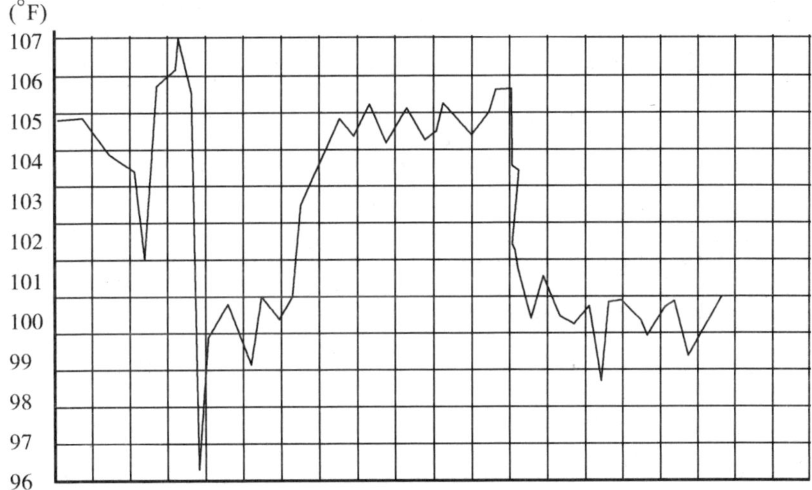

1888年登州府医疗工作报告

聂会东 著

1888年，是我在登州府(Tungchow Fu)连续从事医学工作的第四个年头，这里距离芝罘(Chefoo)约55英里。除了每年的前三个月药房隔天开放外，其余的时间药房每天定时开放。

就诊患者的人数和前几年相比变化不大，冬季就诊患者会少些，到了夏天人数会稍微多一些，大概平均每天接诊13个。今年门诊量为3283人次，其中1396例为初诊。总的来说，在这一年中，无论是外国人还是本地人，其健康状况都相对平稳：往年在8～9月期间发病较高的秋季腹泻，发病率明显下降；今年在芝罘和山东内陆的很多地区发生了严重的甚至是致命的霍乱疫情，但这里霍乱病例很少，据我所知不超过6个；与1887年相比，腹泻和痢疾的发病率也大大降低了。

今年，在我们周围的外国人中没有严重疾病的发生，与我们有工作联系的本地人当中也没有死亡案例发生。

住院患者虽然不是很多，但人数与前几年相比已经有了较大增幅。今年总住院人数是61人，其中治愈43人，11人的病情得到改善，4人的治疗效果不明显，死亡3人。在今年的工作中，我发现，更多的住院患者愿意在医院里多治疗一段时间，以便获得更好的效果；而不像以前，在医院住上几天后如果发现疗效不理想，没有明显的改善，就会对治疗失去信心。对此，我感到非常欣慰。

大多数病人在接受治疗时表现得很焦虑，急切盼望早日康复，但并非所有人都能如愿以偿。也有的人，愿意多花些时间、忍受治疗带来的暂时的痛苦，以获得身体的康复。在我们的治疗措施中，一项值得关注的创新举措是，我们在治疗胃部疾病时采用了洗胃的方法。这种治疗方法需要胃管、漏斗和稀释的碳酸氢钠溶液。通过胃管将稀释的碳酸氢钠溶液输入胃内，以彻底灌洗胃黏膜，中和过多胃酸。我们发现患者能很快接受这种治疗，胃管置管过程也比较顺利，患者往往能够配合做下咽动作；甚至有的患者在了解到洗胃治疗能够减轻他们的痛苦后，会主动要求采用这种治疗方法。

有一个患严重胃黏膜炎的患者，饱受胃痛的折磨，来院时体质消瘦，经过一段时间每日一次的洗胃治疗、饮食调理后，效果良好，几近痊愈，离开医院时体重明显增加。另一位胃酸过多的患者，经过用稀释的苏打水或普通的温水洗胃后，症状得到了明显的缓解，疼痛发作频次及持续的时间都明显减少。但另外一个胃癌患者，洗胃治疗除了使他的疼痛有所减轻外，可以说几乎没有任何作用。

洗胃这一新的治疗方法，或许在一开始会让大家感到工作量比较大，因为需要做一些准备工作，比如要把水温调到 100 ℉，还需要给患者置入胃管。不过经过一段时间后，这些都可以由我们的助理来操作，成为他们的日常工作。洗胃治疗的配方是：水 3 品脱（注：1 品脱＝0.568 升），溶解在 3 德拉克马（注：1 德拉克马＝4.8 克）的碳酸氢钠中。通常 1 德拉克马的碳酸氢钠溶于 1 品脱水中，偶尔的情况下用量会有所增加，但多数情况下用量会有所减少。我是在一篇期刊文章中学到这个治疗方法的，文章作者还推荐了在哪些情况下使用碳酸、硼酸等，或为了得到理想的治疗效果，在什么情况下采用抗发酵治疗，什么情况下使用抗酸治疗。

这一年里，我发现这里的患者对宗教没有表现出明显的兴趣。他们通常会说我们所传授的教义是好的，当我们深入了解他们是否真正理解和接受福音时，有的人甚至说自己信仰上帝。实际上，这个地区的山东人似乎在骨子里是完全排斥任何宗教的。在这个省的一些地方，有些人，尤其是一些女性，似乎在追求精神层面的更高的东西，其中许多人信奉长生不老，其目标是寻求永生。在山东登州这个沿海地区，几乎没有信奉基督教的人。人们都很现实，对超脱世俗的任何事物都不感兴趣。一个人偶尔会有罪恶的想法，这就需要一个救世主，就像贫瘠的土地需要水。

医学教育

这一年里，一个由 5 名学生组成的医学班的教学工作在系统地、有规律地进行着。初夏，他们的第一年学习结束，标志着他们完成了一半的学业，并且通过了包括解剖学、生理学和化学在内的第一次学业考试；秋季，要求他们每周 4 天，每天 2 次温习学过的知识，每周三学习由嘉约翰博士（Dr. Kerr）编写的内科学和手术学方面的教材，年末又通过了一项考试。

今年他们的学业将进入临床实践阶段，学习包括叩诊、听诊在内的患者体格检查方面的知识；同时要求他们定期温习炎症、梅毒、皮肤病等教材上的专业知识；另外还有治疗学、产科学方面的授课。虽然协议上规定学习时间为 3 年，但他们都表示愿意学习到 1890 年夏天过后，这样他们就可以进行为期三年半的医学学习，就会有更多的时间用于内、外科的临床实习。

下面是有关医院和药房今年工作量的统计。

1888 年数据统计

初诊门诊患者	1396	手术	
复诊门诊患者	1887	前臂截肢	1
住院患者	61	拇指截断	1
患者总数	3344	阴茎截断术	1
		肿瘤切除	7
初诊患者所患疾病		肛瘘	2
常见疾病	189	包皮环割术	1
手术	209	针刀棘上韧带松解术	2
呼吸系统疾病	96	肩部手术	1
消化系统疾病	433	腹水抽吸	3
眼、耳疾病	85	脓肿和脓疮引流	14
皮肤疾病	265	骨坏死	1
多系统疾病	119	拔牙	55
共计：1396			

［摘自 *China Medical Missionary Journal*，1889，3(1)］

A Year's Medical Work in Tungchowfu

By James Boyd Neal, M. D.

During 1888, the fourth year of continuous medical work in Tungchowfu, 55 miles from Chefoo. The Dispensary has been kept open regularly every day, except during the first three months of the year, when it was open only on alternate days.

The attendance has been much the same as in former years—small during the cold weather and somewhat larger during the summer—averaging about thirteen cases a day, the total number of visits of out-patients being for the year 3283, of which 1396 were new cases. The year upon the whole was one of unusually good health both among foreigners and natives, especially as regards the usual summer complaints, which are ordinarily so troublesome during August and September. Though there was a severe epidemic of cholera in Chefoo and in many places in the interior of Shantung which proved very fatal, there was little here, not more than half-a-dozen cases being brought to my attention, while the ordinary record of diarrheas and dysenteries was much decreased as compared with 1887.

There has been no dangerous illness among the foreigners of our community, and no deaths among the natives who are connected with us in our work.

The number of hospital patients, though not large, has considerably increased as compared with former years, the whole number being 61, of whom forty-three have been cured, eleven improved, and four unimproved, there having been three deaths during the year. I have been much gratified during this year's work to find an increasing willingness among in-patients to remain in hospital long enough to receive some benefit, instead of becoming discouraged after a few days, if no very evident improvement took place.

Most of them have seemed just as anxious to get well as we have been to help them, which is not always the case, and have been willing to spend time and take pains to effect a cure. The only innovation worthy of note in our practice, has been the use of lavage in treating diseases of the stomach. The treatment consists in daily washing out of the stomach by means of a stomach tube and funnel, with a dilute solution of bicarbonate of soda, so as to thoroughly cleanse the mucous membrane from accumulations of mucus and combat hyperacidity. It is remarkable how quickly a patient becomes accustomed to the passage of the stomach tube, and will swallow it down with almost no difficulty, even coming and asking that it be used, after learning the relief which follows its application.

One case of severe catarrh of the stomach, who on admission was much reduced and suffered greatly from attacks of pain, was almost entirely relieved and left the Dispensary, a fleshy man, after a few weeks of daily washing of his stomach and careful regulation of his diet. Another patient, who suffered from an excessive hyperacidity, was much relieved, and never failed to have a paroxysm of pain cut short by the use of either the dilute soda solution or by lavage with simple tepid water. The treatment however failed to cure him, while another case of cancer of the stomach could scarcely be said to have been benefited at all, though the pain which he complained of was lessened by the washings.

This method of treatment, though a little burdensome at first, owing to the necessity of regulating the temperature of the water to about 100 ℉, and the care required in passing the stomach tube, soon becomes a matter of routine which any ordinary assistant can carry out. The quantity of water used was usually about three pints, having dissolved in it three drachmas of bicarbonate of sodium, though this quantity, of one drachm to each pint of water, was occasionally increased and often diminished, while the Journal from which I learned the method, recommended the use in certain cases of Carbolic Acid, Boric Acid, etc. , when an ant fermentative effect instead of an antacid was desired.

There have been no evidences of any marked religious interest on the part of the patients during the year. They all say the doctrine which we teach is excellent, and some aver that they believe it, but when we look for signs of a real understanding and acceptance of the Gospel they are entirely wanting. The people in this part of Shantung seem to be altogether devoid of any religious element in their character. In some other parts of Shantung, the people, or at least the women, appear to think about higher things and many of them belong to sects whose object is to seek for eternal life, but here in the Shantung Promontory no such spirit exists, the people being all as worldly-minded and as absolutely indifferent to the claims of anything beyond this world as it is possible for them to be. The very occasional case of a man who does grasp the idea of sin and the need of a Savior therefrom, is like water to a thirsty soul in this barren land.

Medical Teaching

The teaching of the medical class of five students has been regularly and systematically carried on during the year. In the early part of the summer, at the end of their first year and a half of study, they passed their first examinations in Anatomy, Physiology and Chemistry, and during the autumn they had recitations twice a day, four days of the week, and once on Wednesday in Dr. Kerr's Practice of Medicine and in Surgery, passing an examination in the latter at the end of the year.

They are going on this year to pursue the study of Practice in conjunction with clinical examination of patients, including percussion and auscultation, having also regular recitations in books on Inflammation, Syphilis, Skin Diseases, etc., and listening to lectures on Therapeutics, Obstetrics, etc. Though they are bound by their contracts to stay only three years, they have all declared themselves willing to remain through the summer of 1890, which will give them a course of three years and a half, and allow them more time to devote to the clinical study of medicine and surgery. Below will be found a short statistical table showing the work for the year in Dispensary and Hospital.

STATISTICS FOR 1888.

New Out-patients	1,396
Old ,, ...	1,887
Hospital ,, ...	61
Total No. of Patients ...	3,344

Diseases of New Patients.

General Diseases	189
Surgical ,, ...	209
Respiratory Tract	96
Alimentary ,, ...	433
Eye and Ear...	85
Skin Diseases	265
Miscellaneous	119
	1,396

List of Operations.

Amputation of Fore-arm ...	1
,, ,, Thumb... ...	1
,, ,, Penis	1
Tumors excised	7
Fistula in Ano	2
Circumcision	1
Needle-and-fish Spine cut out...	2
Shoulder set	1
Ascites tapped...	3
Abscesses and Boils lanced ...	14
Necrosed Bone...	1
Teeth pulled	55

子宫清理手术

聂会东 著

从(音译 Ts'ung)女士,23 岁,结婚 5 年,为了治疗腹部肿瘤于 1889 年 8 月 28 日来到登州诊所。她身体很虚弱,需要别人扶着才能走路,极度贫血和紧张,主诉腹痛明显。

经检查发现,她的子宫扩张明显、阴道闭锁,有一质韧且较厚的纤维性隔膜位于阴道口处并使其完全闭合。她母亲告诉我之前阴道口是通畅的,8 个月前她的女儿出现过外阴疼痛导致其逐渐闭合。

该患者月经停滞,无怀孕史。我在隔膜上做了一长约 1.5 英寸(1 英寸=2.54 厘米)的穿透性切口,发现隔膜 1/8 英寸厚,切开后立即有黏稠的柏油样的液体排出。非常令人惊讶,等流出液相对减少,我伸入手指发现阴道被一个大的、质硬物体占据,进一步检查发现这是一个足月胎儿的头部,颅骨已充分骨化。

我立即准备进行穿颅术,3 个小时后,我成功地把头颅一块一块地取了出来,没有伤及母亲,胎儿的手臂被分开后取出,最后躯干和腿被取出。但是在手术过程中该患者的会阴严重撕裂,几乎被撕裂到腿的边缘,在阴道和直肠间也有轻微的撕裂。胎盘也立即排出了,质地干硬,显然已经从宫体上剥离很长时间了。术后用 1%石炭酸(苯酚)溶液冲洗子宫,创面用碳化棉包扎。冲洗及换药一天进行 2 次,后来一天 3 次,几天之后石炭酸溶液被取代为烧开过的水,每次换药都彻底地冲洗子宫。术后她出现了轻微的感染性发热,持续了九天。第十天在排出了之前的冲洗未能去除的一块坏死组织后,她的体温降至正常。两周后,她食欲旺盛,子宫收缩得很好,几乎没有异物排出。她体力也恢复了,出院回家等待她的身体状况恢复到可以接受会阴手术,因为我在术中并未对会阴撕裂进行彻底的缝合。

（备注:我汇报前面这一病例的目的并不是为了突出阴道闭锁,因为这一现象并不罕见,也不是为了突出穿颅术,而是为了记录以下事实,即直到进行手术后才发现胎儿死亡后在子宫中继续存在了 3 个月。）

这个女人的丈夫 1888 年 8 月去了满洲里(Manchuria)。

大约在春节结束的时候,她开始感觉到胎动,胎动持续到今年阴历的第四个月末(大约 5 月 20 日)分娩痛开始时。经过 10 天徒劳的努力,胎儿没有生下来并停止了活动,显然已经死亡，当地的医生告诉她并没有孩子要出生,她之所以觉得疼痛是由于其他的一些疾病。这名患者说,直到她进入分娩过程几天后她自己检查时,才发现她的阴道是闭合的。她去年十月曾经出现过外阴疼痛,但一直不知道阴道会堵塞。

从这开始,她的子宫时常剧烈疼痛,通常在上午或下午,持续几个小时后缓解,伴随排便困难、膀胱刺激。当她来找我就诊时,孩子的头已经被压入了骨盆并到达阴道口附近,因此她的腹部并不像怀孕的妇女一样大。她的健康尤其是她的血液,由于长期持续的日常痛苦以及从羊水中吸收到的各种有害物质,受到了严重影响。

当我将死婴取出时,没有难闻的气味及腐败迹象,提示子宫被密封达到了气密状态,子宫里残留的羊水是一种稠的、柏油状的液体。如果这位患者的讲述是真实的,那就意味着她的子宫里怀着一个死去的胎儿,这种状态持续了 3 个月,最后她接受了胎儿穿颅术并于术后 2 周回家。然而,这一病例的病史给我印象最深的一件事,就是子宫在经历了长期扩张以及徒劳的分娩以后仍具有的惊人的复原能力。

登州 1889 年 9 月 14 号

[摘自 *China Medical Missionary Journal*, 1889, 3(3)]

Imperforate Vagina-craniotomy

By James Boyd Neal, M. D.

Mrs. Ts'ung, age 23, married five years, presented herself at the Tungchowfu Dispensary, August 28th, 1889, for the relief of a tumor in her abdomen. She was very weak, being unable to walk without assistance, extremely anemic and nervous, and complained of a great deal of pain in her abdomen.

Examination showed her womb much distended, and her vagina imperforate, there being a thick, tough, fibrous septum closing it completely, situated just where its opening should be. Her mother informed me that there had formerly been a passage, but that eight months before, her daughter bad suffered from a sore there, which had caused it to grow shut.

Diagnozing the case as one of retained menses, no history of pregnancy being given, I made an incision, about an inch and a half long, through the septum, which proved to be an eighth of an inch thick, and immediately there was a discharge of thick, tarry-looking matter. Being surprised, however, at the comparative scantiness of the flow, I introduced my finger, and found the vagina occupied by a large, hard body, which, on further examination, proved to be the head of a child at full term, the bones being well ossified.

I immediately set to work to perform craniotomy, and after three hours work succeeded in extracting the head, piece by piece, without tearing the mother. The arms were cut away separately, and finally the trunk and legs were born, but in the effort the woman's perineum was ruptured badly, being torn nearly to the margin of the arms, a slight laceration being also made between the vagina and rectum. The after-birth came away immediately, and was tough and dry, evidently having been detached for a long time. The womb was washed out with 1% carbolic acid solution and the parts dressed with carbonized cotton. This treatment was repeated twice a day, and later on three times a day, boiled water being substituted, after a few days, for the carbolic acid solution, the womb at each dressing being thoroughly washed out. She suffered from slight septic fever for nine days, her temperature dropping to normal on the tenth day, on the coming away of a small piece of foul flesh which had resisted former washings. At the end of two weeks she had developed a hearty appetite, her womb was well contracted, with little discharge, and she had regained her strength sufficiently to return to her home to wait until her physical condition should be such as to warrant an operation on her perineum, the stitches which I put in at the time of the tear failing to cause union.

(*Remarks.* —I have presented the foregoing case not so much to draw attention to the presence of an imperforate vagina, which is not an infrequent occurrence, nor to the performance of craniotomy, but rather to record the following facts, which did not come to light until after the operation, and which seem to indicate the probability of the child having been carried in the womb for three full months after it had died.)

The woman's husband went to Manchuria in the seventh moon of last year, that is, in August 1888.

About the end of the Chinese year she began to feel the foetal movements, which continued until near the end of the fourth moon of this year (approximately May 20th), when labor pains set in. After ten days of ineffectual efforts to expel the child, the foetus ceased its movements, having apparently died, the native doctors all telling her that she had no child to be born, the pains she was suffering being due to some other trouble. The woman herself says she was not aware that her vagina was closed until after she had been in labor some days, when on examining herself she found no opening. She had had a soreness about her vulva, in October of last year, but had not known that it had grown over.

From this time on she suffered from very severe pains in her womb, coming on either in the morning or afternoon and continuing several hours, then ceasing, from great difficulty in defecation, and from irritability of her bladder. When she came to me, the head of the child was pressed low down into the pelvis, being near the opening of the vagina, her abdomen was not nearly so much distended as is usual at term, while her general health, and especially her blood, had suffered severely, from the long-continued strain of daily suffering, and from absorption of the contents of the bag of waters. When I removed the child there was no offensive odor whatsoever and no signs of putrefaction, showing that the womb bad been sealed up airtight, while the remains of the amniotic fluid was a thick, tarry-like liquid. If the woman's story is a true one, she had carried a dead child in her womb for three months, and yet at the end of that time was able to submit to the operation of craniotomy and return to her home in two weeks. The thing, however, which impressed me most in the history of the case was the ability which the womb displayed of going through its course of involution so rapidly after so long a period of distention and vain efforts at expulsion.

Tungchowfu, *September* 14*th*, 1889.

论医学生培养及其成功前景

聂会东 著

对于让我讨论的这个课题我非常感兴趣，虽然向同事们提出自己关于医学教学的观点有点心虚，毕竟我在中国的时间不长，但我还是想就这个主题写点东西。在我来这里之前，我就对培养本地医生感兴趣，正因如此我被邀请到山东从事这项工作，一到这里，我就直接投入这项工作中了。前三年我一直致力于教学准备工作，在过去的 3 年里，我为 5 名年轻人开设了医学课，进行系统的医学课程学习。回顾了我在这方面或多或少的经验后，我下面将简要地讨论这个问题。

1. 学制

以我的经验，用令人满意的方式培养学生，最重要的是要有充裕的时间。这样一来，他们不仅可以对既定的知识学习 1～2 次，还有时间去复习和回顾课程，而且在有书籍的情况下，除了定期复习课和讲座，还有时间进行课外阅读。我开始利用 3 年的时间举办培训课程，但课程进行了不到一半的时候，我觉得不太可能在既定的时间内完成这项任务，或许只有通过不寻常的努力才有可能完成，只好让他们再多学习半年以通过课程，并给他们提供必要的机会进行临床实习。即使在最有利的情况下，也无法实现每年进行 8～9 个月的系统教学。考虑到医生的时间和精力，能有 7 个月不间断的时间来做这项工作已经是很幸运了。因此，我认为医学学习的时间最少应该是 4 年，如把物理、历史、地理等基础学习加入在课程中，5 年的时间也不算多。除了固定一个明确的学期之外，我认为教师也应根据教学时间为自己制定一些规则。山东长老会最近采纳了这项规定，要求 4 年的学习中，每年教学时间至少 7 个月。这似乎是系统教学最合适的时间，我们当然希望学生能好好利用每学年剩余的5个月，照顾住院病人，聆听临床教学，特别是在课程后期更应如此。关于常规教学时间，因为每个人的情况是不一样的，所以没有一个普遍的规则可以制定。我自己的习惯是一周8次诵读或讲座，分别是在星期一、星期二、星期四、星期五的上午和下午；学生也须隔日轮流在诊所当助手，并在临床实践时接受指导。这使他们相当忙碌，但也有空闲时间进行必要的记录，以及完成其他杂项职责。

当然，我很清楚，我在登州的情况是特殊的，随着实践工作和外部需求的增加，我可能会发现，完全不可能把这么多时间专门用于教学。但是，如果有一个合格的助手协助我教学的话，每周8次的诵读是完全可以实现的。甚至在学生们还没有准备好临床工作的前1～2年还会有更多的诵读课程。

2. 教学语言

尽管最近在《教务杂志》上一位作者强烈呼吁用英语教授外国知识，并对这种教学方式的顺利进行及成功前景持乐观态度。我越来越确信和坚定，在远离港口的地方，我们传教士应该使用的语言是中文。确定一个固定的命名制度后，我相信我们不久便可以用汉语表达我们在医学教学中想传达的所有思想。我并不反对愿意花时间来教英语的人，特别是在目前好的书籍稀缺，以及系统命名法尚未确定的情况下，任何一个学生都不可能仅凭对中文书籍的学习就能获得英文书籍中那么多的医学知识，我认为我们应该尽最大的努力来建立一套合适的术语，并构建一套本土的医学书籍，这可以使中国人用自己的语言获得知识。除了那些有充分时间和足够财力的人，可以花上几年的时间来学习英语，甚至还可以出国学习，我不相信中国人单纯为了获取知识愿意去阅读英文书籍而掌握英语的能力。我们当中不少人已经花了六七年的时间学习汉语，但是有多少人能在不需要老师或字典帮助的情况下，拿起一本书来读时感觉毫不费力？对于中国人，在周围的人不断地说着与他们所学语言不同的语言，也没有机会在日常生活中运用自己掌握的英语的情况下，能阅读英文的人何其少？我认为，用英语学习医学只局限于少数人，他们有自己的资源，而那些来教会医院受教的人却几乎没有这种资源。

我也认为,教学应该尽可能使用教科书并且定期背诵,而不是通过讲座的形式。我们自己国内的医学教育通过讲座的方式,不仅枯燥,而且对于大多数学生来说,他们在讲座中的收益与所花费的宝贵时间不成正比。很多次我在想,相比于在医学课程中听一场关于实践的枯燥的讲座,我在房间里阅读一个小时课本能获取更多的知识。这里的学生也不习惯记笔记,授课是一项缓慢而乏味的工作,为了保证对自己所学的知识完全理解,需要大量的重复记忆和背诵。

另外,我认为,在编写中文教科书时,我们应该做到尽可能地认真,尤其是我们建议印刷并提供给别人用于教学的教科书。没有什么比发现印刷的书本有很多错误更让人伤脑筋的了,因为它实际上毫无用处,除非被纠正过来,或者过于简洁,使其有必要通过讲座和解析来对这本书进行补充。我们应该努力做好我们能够做到的一切,因为这关系到我们自己和作为中国教师的声誉。在翻译一些在英国和美国出版的优秀教科书方面,有志人士可以大展宏图,我们能够胜任的博医会成员越早全身心地投入翻译工作越好。只有用一流的汉语水平用心地工作,才不会制造出让受过良好教育的中国人所不能容忍的粗陋文字作品,而令我们自己和我们的事业蒙羞。

3. 学习课程

我们的目标应该是使中国医学生学习的课程与美国医学院和课程一样全面,系统地将课程划分为 4 年或 5 年,使我们的毕业生在工作之前完全具备工作能力。当然我们不能指望像西方国家多年来所做的那样进行解剖学和病理学的学习,但通过使用模型和教具、动物解剖,我相信可以让学生获得良好的解剖学知识,而且,通过使用保存的标本,至少可以获得一些实用的病理知识。对于组织学课程,我认为没有必要像美国一样在实验室里做细致和实际的工作,但对于化学的学习,我想提出一个特别的请求。我对这个学科特别感兴趣,我认为只有通过在实验室里实际操作才能获得有用的化学知识。我现在已经开始上课了,课程包括几个月至一年的实验室操作,教他们常见的元素反应、分析无机化合物，最后研究一下身体重要的分泌物和排泄物，比如胃液、胰液、胆汁、尿液等。

我觉得要特别强调基础科目的学习(如解剖学、生理学、化学、药学)，在让学生学习更深入的东西之前，要让学生彻底地了解这些基础性的东西。在这些研究上花费整整两年都不会是浪费时间。

在学到更实用的学科如外科、实践、皮肤疾病和眼部疾病时，我们肯定有一个无与伦比的实践教学领域。我敢断言，如果一个中国学生充分利用他的临床学习机会，他的指导医师也能够认真地利用他手中的案例。相比美国的医学院，他可能会在上述除了外科急诊的学科中获得更多的实践知识。因为美国的医学院人数众多而拥挤，缺乏独立给病人做检查的机会。我们最大的困难在于中国学生在有机会自己学习案例时的落后与保守，他们显然缺乏美国学生所拥有的渴望学习的热情。在这里，年轻人似乎仅仅满足于摆在他们面前的学习任务，在所有事情上都等待着指导医师的引导，显然无法为自己做规划，或者独立思考。这使我开始思考本文的第四部分，即合作教学。

4. 合作教学

我们许多人被分派独自工作，附近也没有同事，要想实现共同教学都需要花费几天的路程，因此我们面临一个严峻的问题：如何对学生进行多样化的教学，接受来自不同导师的指导？

毫无疑问，最好的解决办法是让两个或更多的医生在同一个地方工作，互相补充，每个人都教授那些他觉得最有趣的学科。为了达到培训医生的目的，同一教会的不同工作站之间进行合作，甚至是在一个特定省所有医生联合，不管教会之间的差异。在大多数情况下，这是不可能实现的。然而，这些是在目前不太满意的情况下对可能采取的合作方式的一些建议。

我们期待未来一段时间在中国不同地区建立实力强大、装备精良的医学院，学生可以被送去接受系统的医学训练，这不是任何一个或两个人就能够给予他们的。我认为没有多样化的教学，就不能指望培养出优秀的内科医生和外科医生。一个人，不管他自己有多优秀，或者有多么努力地为他的学生提供全面的训练，在兼顾医疗工作的同时，也不能完成教学过程中所有他应该做的事。同样，让学生想法活跃，给他们多方面观点，从昏昏欲睡中激励他们，让他们独立思考，这种多元化思想的影响力是培养年轻人承担医疗职业责任和依靠自身造诣和独创性处理状况的最重要的因素。我希望在许多情况下，我们的学生在行医过程中能够脱离外国医生和在疑难病例中有资格对他们提供帮助的同行。在没有书籍可以参考的时候，我们为那些没有学会思考和自我计划的人感到悲哀。

5. 培养医学生的目的

我们培训医生的目的是帮助处于苦难中的人，帮助同胞获得身体健康，没有人会否认这一主张，这是一件高尚而有价值的事情。但是我想我们作为福音传教士，应该有一个更高的目标，即在精神方面引导他们成为同胞的精神导师。我并不是提倡医学教育中加入神学培训，我认为两者应该是完全独立的，但是在我们与学生的交往中，在我们祈祷学生的成功时，我们应该不断地在我们的观点和他们的观点中保持基督教显著影响的重要性。因此，我认为我们应尽量训练基督徒，或者至少让基督教元素在我们的课程中占主导地位，除了每日敬拜，定期举办祈祷会，鼓励他们与病人交谈，并在各方面努力灌输传教士的精神，让他们明白我们期待他们大放光彩。虽然他们可能不会做一些传教工作，但这取决于他们谋生的职业，我们仍真诚地希望他们能尝试着引导别人了解福音，就像他们是为这个目的受雇佣的一样。我对培养医学生的期望，不是他们将会成为教会医院的帮手，或是以任何其他身份被外国人雇佣，而是从同胞中走出来，在他们中间传播福音，依靠他们的实践支持，并抓住每一个机会传播宗教。如果我们为此目的培养人，把他们作为独立的工作者派遣出去，我认为给他们最好的医学指导更为重要，而不是把他们培养成在外国人监督下的教会医院助手。

毫无疑问一定比例的毕业生将会应聘成为外国人的助理，因为他们对我们是不可或缺的，在某些情况下将医院完全委托给他们，使他们成为真正的医学传教士也是明智的，但我认为这些情况只应是少数，而我们的目标应该是建立一个本土的医学会，贯穿基督精神，使他们能独立工作。但是这样培养出的独立工作者，除非我们能为他们提供一本用他们自己语言编写的期刊，让他们了解医学科学和实践的最新进展，否则不能奢望看到他们在医学知识和技能方面的进步。为此，我衷心地提出创办中文医学杂志的建议。这样的出版物不仅有助于青年人与时俱进，而且也是教师和学生之间的交流媒介，这是非常可取的。此外，还可以培养中国不同地区国外医学实践者的团队精神，这在未来会成为他们的共同优势。这样的期刊，可以大部分由国外医学期刊翻译而来的文章组成，再辅以在中国从业的外国人、国内毕业医学生的文章。这样组合成的出版物不仅能够给那些学习西医的人提供支持，还能为许多渴望学习国外的实践方法的本土教师提供支持。

6. 成功前景

我的这篇论文恐怕有些冗长，或许我应该将最后的这部分内容留给那些更有经验的，更权威的人进行探讨。顺便说一句，我知道登州有三四个人从事西医实践，除一人外，所有人都比初级的医学毕业生做得更好，尽管他们中没有一个人受过全面的训练，仅仅是通过在医院协助外国医师的实践中获得知识。如此看来，如果这些人能够成功，那么，那些精力充沛并且为实践做好准备的人，至少能做到同样的好。

[摘自 *China Medical Missionary Journal*, 1889, 3(3)]

Training of Medical Students and Their Prospects

The subject which has been assigned to me for discussion, is one in which I am deeply interested, and though I feel somewhat different about offering my ideas, upon medical teaching to my colleagues, after so short an experience in China, yet there is no other theme upon which I should prefer to write. Before coming to the foreign field my attention directed to the subject of training native doctors, and I was invited to Shantung more particularly to engage in such work, so that from my arrival on the field my thoughts have been directed in that channel. My first three years wore devoted to preparation for teaching, and the past three years to the carrying on of a medical class of five young men through a systematic graded course of medical study. Now having premised just how much, and just how little experience, I have had in this line, I shall proceed to briefly discuss the question.

Ⅰ. *Length of Course*

The one lesson above all others which my experience has taught me is, that in order to train students in a satisfactory manner, abundance of time must be allowed, so that not only may it be possible to take them over a settled line of studies once or twice, but so that they may have leisure to review and re-review, and in cases where there are collateral books, may have time to do outside reading, in addition to the regular recitations and lectures. I started out to take a class through in three years, but had not half exhausted the time, when I saw how impossible it would be to accomplish the task in the time allotted, and only by unusual effects will it be possible, by keeping them another half-year, to put them through the course, and give them the opportunities for clinical instruction which they should have. Under the most favorable circumstances, it impossible to give more than eight or nine months of each year to systematic teaching, and when the extra calls upon a physician's time and strength arc taken into account, he may count himself fortunate if he is able to secure seven months of uninterrupted time for such work. So that I think the minimum of time which should be allowed for medical study should be four years and if it intended to include any preliminary studies, such as Physics, History, Geography, etc. , in the course, five years would not be too much. In addition to this fixing upon a definite term of years to be spent in study, I think it is well for the instructor to also lay down certain rules for himself, in regard to the amount of time he will give to teaching. The rule, which has lately adopted by the Shantung Presbyterian Mission, requires four years of study, of at least seven months' teaching in each year. This seems a fair proportion of time to be given to systematic instruction, the students of course being expected to spend a goodly portion of the remaining five months, especially during the latter part of their course, in care of the sick in hospital, and in listening to occasional clinical teaching. With regard to the amount of time to be given each week during the regular terms to the teaching, no doubt no two men's circumstances and engagements are alike, so that no general rule can be laid down. My own habit is to have eight recitations or lectures a week, one in the morning and one in the afternoon on Monday, Tuesday, Thursday and Friday; the students being also required to assist in the Dispensary on alternate days, and to receive instruction clinically as occasion serves. This keeps them fairly busy, yet allows them time for recreation, and for necessary copying of notes, and for other miscellaneous duties.

I am quite aware of course, that my circumstances in Tungchowfu have been exceptional, and that with a larger practice on my hands and more outside demands upon my time, I might find it quite impossible to give so many course exclusively to teaching. I think, however, with a properly qualified assistant, who could help in the teaching, it might be possible to require as many as eight recitations per week, or possibly more during the first year or two, when the students are not yet prepared for clinical work.

Ⅱ. *Medium of Instruction*

Notwithstanding the strong plea lately made by a writer in the *Chinese Recorder*, for the teaching of foreign sciences in English, and the sanguine views he took of the ease with which such teaching could be carried on, and the prospect of success which would attend it, I cannot help but feel more and more convinced that the medium which we as missionaries should use, especially in places remote from the ports, is the Chinese. With a settled system of nomenclature, which I feel sure we shall not be long in securing, the Chinese language, I believe, can be made to express all the ideas which we wish to convey in the teaching of Medicine. I would by no means decry the use of English by those who are willing to spend the time necessary to teach it, for certainly in the present scarcity of good books, and the unsettled state of the nomenclature, no student can hope to obtain so thorough a knowledge of medicine by the study of Chinese books alone, as he can by the use of English, but I think we should use our utmost endeavor to fix upon a suitable set of terms, and build up a native medical literature, which shall enable a Chairman to attain to perfection as nearly in his own language as in English. Except in the case of those who have unlimited time and money at their disposal, so enable them to spend years in the acquisition of English, and perhaps go abroad to pursue their studies, I have no faith in the ability of the Chinese to so master English as to be able and willing to read English books for the pure pleasure of acquiring knowledge. How many of us, who have spent the best part of six or seven years in the study of Chinese, feel sufficiently familiar with it to pick up a book and read it for pleasure, without either teacher or dictionary to help us? and how much less the Chinese in the reading of English. who, surrounding by people constantly speaking a language different from that which they are studying, have not the same incentive to apply themselves and master the English for daily use. I conceive that the study of Medicine in English must always be confined to the favored few, who have resources at their command, such as almost none of those who come to be taught in Mission hospitals have.

I think too, that teaching should be done as much as possible by the use of text-books and by regular recitations, rather than by lectures. The system of medical education at home, by means of lectures, is not only a bore, but for the majority of students entails an expenditure of valuable time, out of all proportion to the amount of benefit derived from the lectures. Many times have I thought, while listening to a dry lecture on Practice during my medical course, how much more I could absorb from an hour with a good text-book in my own room, than I was getting from him. Here too, where students are unaccustomed to taking notes, the delivery of lectures is very slow and tedious work, involving a large amount of repetition, and reiteration, in order to insure a full understanding of the subject in hand.

Again, I think we can not be too careful in the preparation of text-books in Chinese, especially of those which we propose to have printed and offer to others for use in teaching. Nothing is so vexatious to find a printed book so full of mistakes, as to be practicality useless, until gone over and corrected, or so elementary in the treatment of a subject, as to make it necessary to supplement the book largely by lectures and explanations. We owe it to ourselves and our own reputation as teachers of the Chinese, to strive to put forth nothing but what is as good as it is possible for us to make it. In the line of translations of some of the many excellent text-books, now issued in England and America, there is a wide field open to those who are fitted for such work, and the sooner more of the members of our Medical Missionary Association, who are qualified for it enter heartily into the work of translation the better, only let us by all means have good, honest work and first-rate Chinese, let us not disgrace ourselves and dishonor our cause by sending out slipshod productions in language, which no well-educated Chairman will tolerate.

Ⅲ. *Course of Study*

It should be our aim to make the course of study for Chinese medical students, as thorough and comprehensive as in the medical schools at home, dividing the studies among the four or five years in a systematic way, and endeavoring to send our graduates out thoroughly equipped for the work before them. Of course we can not hope to pursue the study of Anatomy and Pathology, as done in the West for many years to come, but by the use of models and preparations, and dissection of animals, I believe it is possible to give men here a good knowledge of Anatomy, and, by the use of preserved specimens, at least some practical information about Pathology. In the line of Histology, I see no reason why as careful and practical work in laboratory, should not be done here as at home, while for the study of Chemistry, I should like to make a special plea. Being particularly interested in this branch, and believing only by practical work in the laboratory can a useful knowledge of Chemistry be gained, I have taken my present classes through a course of several months or a year of laboratory practice, teaching them the reactions of the more common elements and the analysis of inorganic compounds, and closing with a study of the more important secretions and excretions of the body, such as the gastric juice, pancreatic juice, bile, urine, etc.

Upon all, of what may be called the foundation studies, such as Anatomy, Physiology, Chemistry and Materia Medicine, I feel like having special stress, grounding the students thoroughly in these, before carrying them on to the higher branches. Two full years spent upon these studies would certainly not be lost time.

When we come to the more practical branches of Surgery, Practice, Diseases of the Skin, and of the Eye, we certainly have an unrivalled field for practical teaching. I do not hesitate to say that if a student makes the most of his opportunities for clinical study, and his preceptor is careful in making use of the cases which come to his hand, he may gain a wider practical knowledge of the branches mentioned above, except of course, emergency Surgery, than in many of the crowded medical schools at home, where the member of students is so large, that each individual has comparatively scanty opportunities of examining patients for himself. The great difficulty lies in the backwardness of Chinese students in availing themselves of chances which come to them of studying cases for themselves, they, apparently lacking the enthusiasm which many students at home possess, and which makes them eager to learn. Here, young men seem content to learn simply the task set before them, waiting for the leading of the preceptor in all things being apparently incapable of marking out work for themselves, or of doing independent thinking. This brings me to the consideration of the fourth division of my subject, namely,—

Ⅳ. *Co-operation in Teaching*

Many of us being stationed alone, without any colleague within several days journey who can take part with us in teaching, it becomes a serious question how to give our students that variety of instruction, and that stimulus, which comes from listening to different instructors.

The best solution of the difficulty no doubt is, to have two or more physicians associated in work in the same place, mutually supplementing each other, and each teaching those branches in which he feels the liveliest interest. But in many cases this is impossible, and then comes the alternative of co-operation between different stations of the same Mission, or even a grand combination of all the physicians in a given province, regardless of differences between Missions, for the purpose of training medical men. These, however, are only suggestions of what may be done in the way of co-operation now, in the present unsatisfactory state of affairs.

No doubt we all look forward to a time in the future when strong and well-equipped medical schools will be found in different parts of the empire, to which students may be sent to receive that thorough training in medicine, which it is impossible for anyone or any two men alone to give them. Nothing is more certain to my mind that the fact that without variety in teaching we cannot hope to produce well-rounded-out physicians and surgeons. No one man, no matter how good he may be himself, nor how diligent in striving to give his students a thorough training, can do everything in the way of teaching, that should be done, and at the same time attend to his medical work. Then too, the influence of more than one mind upon students in quickening their perceptions and in giving them many-sided views, waking them up from their lethargy and inspiring them to think for themselves, is a most important element in the training of young men to enter upon the responsibilities of the medical profession, in circumstances where they will have to rely solely upon their own attainments and their native ingenuity. In some, I hope many cases, our students in practicing for themselves will be far removed from foreign physicians and from fellow-practitioner qualified to help them in difficult cases, and then woe to the man who, with few or no books to consult, has never learned to think and plan for himself.

Ⅴ. *Object in Teaching Medical Students*

No one probably will gainsay the proposition, that the training of medical men with the purpose study of fitting them to minister to suffering people, and this help their fellows physically, is a noble and worthy object. But we as missionaries of the Gospel, I think, should have a still higher aim in view, namely, the training of men to be teachers of their countrymen in spiritual things. Not that I would advocate the tacking on of a theological training upon a medical education, for I think the two should be kept entirely separate and distinct, but that in our intercourse with our students and in our prayers for their success, we should keep constantly in our view, and in theirs, the prime importance of their exerting a marked influence for Christianity. For this reason I think it is well for us as far as possible to train Christians, or at least to have the Christian dement in our classes decidedly dominant, to have regular meetings for prayer with them, aside from the daily worship, to encourage them to talk with patients, and in every way endeavor to instill into them the spirit of missionaries, making them understand that we look to them to let their light shine, and that though they may not be connected with the Mission in doing direct missionary work, but depending simply upon their profession for a living, yet we expect them to be as earnest in trying to lead others to a knowledge of the Gospel, as if they were employed for the purpose. My own hope in training medical students is not that they will become helpers in Mission hospitals, or enter into the employ of foreigners in any other capacity, but that they will go out among their countrymen, and *line* the Gospel among them, depending upon their practice for support, and taking every opportunity to speak a word for their religion. If we train men with this end in view, of sending them out as independent workers, I think it is even more important to give them the very best of medical instruction, than it would be if we were fitting them to be simply helpers in mission dispensaries, where they would be under the supervision of foreigners.

No doubt a certain proportion of our graduates will always be employed assistants to foreigners, as they are indispensable to us, and in certain cases it may be advisable to entrust dispensaries entirely to their care, making them real medical missionaries, but I think these cases should be the exception, and that our aim should be to build up a native medical fraternity, thoroughly Christian in spirit, and independent in its workings. But in thus sending out men to be independent practitioners, we can not hope to see them progress in medical knowledge and skill, unless we give them a journal in their own language, devoted to keeping them informed in regard to the advances of medical science and practice. For this reason I am most heartily interested in the proposal to start a medical journal in Chinese. Such a publication would serve not only to keep the young men up to the times, but would also be a medium of communication between teachers and former pupils, which would be very desirable. Moreover it would foster a certain esprit de corps among men practicing foreign medicine in different parts of China, which in the future might be very much to their mutual advantage. Such a journal, I conceive, insight be made up in part, perhaps in large part, of translations from foreign medical periodicals, and these translations, supplemented by articles from foreign practitioners in China, and from native medical graduates, might be combined into a publication which would command the support of not only those who are practicing foreign medicine, but also of many of the native faculty, who are anxious to learn a little about foreign methods of practice.

Ⅵ. *Prospects of Success*

My paper, I fear, is already too long, so I shall have the discussion of this part of the subject, to those who have had a longer experience and therefore can speak more authoritatively upon it, merely remarking in passing, that of the three or four natives whom I know to be practicing foreign medicine in this region of Tungchowfu, all, with possibly one exception, are making more than graduates of the first degree can command, and this despite the fact that not one of them has received a thorough training, having merely picked up what they know, through assisting foreigners in dispensary practice. It would seem that if these men can succeed, surely men of energy and devotion, who have faithfully prepared themselves for practice ought to be able to do at least equally well.

山东的医学工作

聂会东 著

在山东省长老会的6个站点中,除了芝罘(Chefoo)作为本省港口城市能够得到外来医疗服务之外,其他站点都配有一名医生,并且其中的4个站点还有一位女医生。除了芝罘外,每个站点都有每日药房和医院为中国人提供诊疗服务,许多中国人因此受益;另外我们还时常在站点外的各地进行医疗巡回活动。

在所有的站点,医疗工作的运营费用都是由差会出资维持的,但是,其中有3个站点的主要建筑则是由私人捐赠或私人遗产购买修建的。比如,潍县(Wei Hien)的两家医院(男子医院和女子医院)建设资金就是为纪念阿撒拉(Sarah Archibald Mateer)女士的生活和工作筹集而来的;济宁州(Chi-ning Chow)的医院是由私人捐赠的;济南府文璧(McIlvaine)医院是用牧师文璧(Rer. Jasper McIlvaine)留下的遗产建造而成的,他于1881年在济南的工作岗位上去世。在登州府(Tengchowfu)和沂州府(Ichowfu)的两个传教点,医疗工作在传教会租用的房屋内进行。

在全省,医疗工作人员的目标是使医院既成为直接和间接传播福音的机构,同时又可以细致、令人满意地治疗疾病。我认为,无论医生多么希望看到中国人病情好转,如果他在传教工作上没有取得成功,他就不是成功的传教士。在每一家医院和诊所,我们都努力向病人传播教义,或是向正在等待治疗的患者布道交谈,抑或在患者住院期间对他们进行传教。至于以这种方式传教可以取得的效果,则是难以估计的。在中国的传教士们普遍认为,在每日诊所里,患者只待很短的时间,也许永远不会回来,传教工作几乎没有什么可察觉的效果。然而,我们认为,这样的工作对于打破人们的偏见,让人们对提供这种慈善机构的人产生亲切感是有一定效果的。尤其在中国还有大量的工作需要做，以纠正人们对于我们这些他们口中的“洋鬼子”的陈旧迂腐的思想观念，似乎没有什么比医疗工作更能吸引他们对我们的支持和赞同了。

各地的人们都渴望得到西医医疗服务，在一些基本不可能得到他们对基督教尊重的地方，人们将成群结队前来求治各种疾病。在医院里，传教的结果是非常令人鼓舞的，尽管仍然有点令人不满意。一旦有几天的时间，或者幸运的话几周的时间，我们有机会定期指导病人并向他们传播基督教义，我们就有机会留下他们进行传教，直到他们离开医院。即使我们没有让人们的信仰转变，常常让我们感到欣慰的是，在患者住院期间，人们越来越友好、有信心，对我们的怀疑也减少了。有时，看到患者接受并信仰基督教，或许还能在他们居住的地方产生相当的影响，我们的心倍感温暖。有报道，1892 年在潍县(Wei Hien)的一家医院，一位年轻人转信基督教，他回到 100 英里(1 英里＝1.609 千米)外的家里，告知人们他的信念，结果 16 个人信仰基督教，并组成家庭教会。自从我上次从美国回来后，我对一位老年患者的来访感到欣慰，老人两年前因断腿而接受治疗，他真诚地皈依了基督教并加入济南府(Chinanfu)的基督教会。他是一个自尊心很强的铁匠，在一个遥远的小镇上工作，显然他仍然真诚地信仰基督教。

从我们的医疗工作中，我们得到了所希冀的精神成果，对收获感到非常欣慰。作为医生，我们感觉到仅仅是为了一些直观的结果——治愈疾病、减轻一些中国当地医生完全无法缓解的痛苦，这项工作也是值得做的。1893 年，在山东的 5 家诊所里，总共有近 5 万来访人次，大约有 3 万名患者。除去那些不愿为治疗付出努力而病情没有好转的人，仍然有大量的患者在治疗中或多或少受益。在这片土地上，短期的经验已经足以让人们看到西医的实用之处，不仅是治疗严重的外科疾病，而且可以简单地教会人们如何护理他们的皮肤和眼睛。人们经常为眼部疾病和皮肤病的困扰而感到痛苦，其实如果多加注意的话，这类疾病是很容易被治愈的。

还有一个有趣的领域，它既不同于日常医疗工作，也不同于传播福音，摆在了山东教会面前——承担着培养年轻医生的任务。到目前为止，只有 11 个或 12 个人受过这样的训练，其中 4 个人还在接受培训，但是几个月后便可以开始工作。这项工作的目的不仅仅是培养为诊所工作的医务人员，更是培养年轻的基督教医生团体。他们中的大多数人最终会走出去，扎根于人民当中，以医学专业为支撑，不仅会使人们受益于西医治疗，并且还将以基督教的生活不断影响并感化人们加入基督教。从那些已经尝试过这个培训的人的经验来看，以西医为谋生手段，他们拥有美好的前途。因此，如果我们能使我们的学生（他们目前都是基督教徒）牢记在离开我们后仍须坚持温暖虔诚的基督徒生活的必要性，那么培养独立的医务人员，似乎是我们面前一个最广泛、最吸引人的领域。

（摘自 *The Church at Home and Aboard Relating to China and Chinese*, 1894-1896, VoL. 4）

Medical Work in Shantung.

By James Boyd Neal, M. D.

Of the six stations of the Presbyterian Board in the province of Shantung, China, all except that at Chefoo, the port of the province where outside medical advice is available, are supplied with a medical man for each station, and in four of them there is also a lady physician. In every station except Chefoo there is also daily dispensary and hospital practice carried on for the benefit of the Chinese who largely patronize such institutions, and in addition more or less medical itinerating among outside country stations is done from time to time.

In all the stations the supplies and running expenses of the medical work are paid out of the treasury of the Board, but in three of the stations the necessary buildings have been erected or bought with funds contributed by private individuals or left by legacy. For instance the two hospitals at Wei Hien, for men and women, have been built from a fund collected for the purpose of commemorating the life and work of Mrs. Sarah Archibald Mateer; the hospital at Chining Chow is also a gift of private individuals; while the McIlvaine Hospital at Chinanfu has been built from a legacy left by Rev. Jasper McIlvaine, who died at his post here in Chinanfu in 1881. In the other two stations, Fengchowfu and Ichowfu, medical work is carried on in premises rented by the Board.

Throughout the province it is the aim of those who have charge of the medical work to make it both a direct and an indirect agency in the evangelization of the Chinese, as well as to do careful and satisfactory work in the way of healing disease. It has always been the writer's feeling that no matter how earnest a doctor might be in his desire to see the Chinese converted and to do them good himself, if he did not make a success of his profession, he thus far failed of being a success as a missionary. At each hospital and dispensary direct efforts are made to bring the truth to the hearing of the patients, either through preaching and talking to the daily patients while waiting to be treated, or by conversation with and teaching of the patients while in hospital. As to the amount of good accomplished in this way it is almost impossible to form any estimate. It is the universal testimony of missionaries in China that the daily dispensary work, where patients are seen for only a few moments, and perhaps never return, yields very little perceptible fruit. And yet it is impossible to think that such work is not without large results in the way of breaking down prejudice and inclining the people to feel kindly toward those who provide such benevolent institutions. In China especially an immense amount remains to be done in disabusing the minds of the people of false and foolish notions in regard to the intentions of "foreign devils", as they still persist in calling us, and nothing seems to appeal to them and enlist their sympathy so truly as medical work.

The people everywhere are keen in their desire for foreign medicine, and in places where it may be impossible to obtain a respectful hearing for the Gospel they will come in numbers to be treated for their various ailments. In hospital practice the results for Christianity are much more encouraging, though still a little disappointing. Where for some days, or still better for some weeks, we have the opportunity to regularly instruct patients and drill them in the principles of the Gospel, there is far more chance of obtaining a hold upon them which will not relax the instant they leave the hospital. Even in cases where we cannot rejoice in any evidences of conversion it is often gratifying to see the increased friendliness and confidence and allaying of suspicion which has been brought about by a stay in hospital. Sometimes our hearts are warmed by seeing patients come out openly and make a good confession of their faith in Christ and perhaps become centers of influence in the regions where they live. In the report from the Wei Hien Hospital for 1892 is cited the case of a young man converted while in a hospital, who went back to his home, nearly a hundred miles away, and told of his faith to such good purpose that a church of sixteen members was gathered together in his house. Since the writer's late return from America he has been gratified by a visit from an old patient, who was treated over two years ago for a broken leg, and who seemed sincerely converted and united with the church in Chinanfu. He is a self-respecting blacksmith, working at his trade in a distant town, and apparently still sincere in his Christian life.

Much as we may desire such spiritual results from our medical work, and heart warming as they are when they do come, as physicians we cannot but feel that the work is worth doing simply for its visible results in the curing of disease and the alleviating of some of the miseries which the native Chinese practitioners are utterly incapable of relieving. During 1893 at our five daily dispensaries in Shantung there were in all nearly 50 000 visits paid, representing perhaps 30 000 patients. Even eliminating those who would take no pains to follow directions in the use of remedies and would thus fail to receive any good, there still remains a large number who must have been benefited more or less by the treatment received. A very short experience in this land is sufficient to persuade one of the usefulness of foreign medical practice, not only in relieving the more serious surgical diseases but simply in teaching the people how to care for their skin and their eyes. One is often saddened by the ravages of eye troubles and skin diseases, which if they had not been neglected might easily have been cured.

An interesting side field, distinct from the daily medical work and from the evangelistic side of the question, is opening up before the Shantung Mission in the line of training up young men to practice medicine on their own account. Up to the present only some eleven or twelve have been so trained, and of these, four are still under instruction, but will be ready for work in a few months. The aim of those most interested in this undertaking is not merely to train up medical helpers for use in our various dispensaries, but to also develop a body of young Christian doctors, most of whom will eventually go out and settle among their own people and, relying upon their profession for support, will not only benefit the Chinese by giving them foreign medical treatment, but will also influence them towards Christianity by a consistent Christian life. The prospects, so far as can be judged from the experience of those who have already tried the experiment, seem good for the making of a comfortable livelihood from the practice of medicine, so that if we can so impress upon our students, all of whom so far have been Christians, the necessity of living a warm, earnest Christian life after they leave us, the field open before us in the line of training independent medical men seems a most broad and inviting one.

医学传教士的科研机会

聂会东 著

去年秋天，我坐着马车，一路颠簸去参加在距离济南府(Chinanfu)150英里的潍县(Wei Hien)举办的差会年会。这几天，我一路看着窗外的这个国家，有一个想法强烈冲击着我：我们医学传教士拥有如此大的机会能为世界的科学观察做些事情，这不仅是有趣的，而且是非常有价值的。

我们在中国的领域是如此广阔，而且几乎没有人探索过这个领域，这几乎是一个拥有无限探索可能性的处女地。我们只有这么几个人，分散在这个帝国的各个地方，几乎无法从日常工作中抽出一点时间来去从事科学工作。然而，我们之中也有许多人在化学、矿物学、地质学、气象学或植物学方面有过些许专业训练，因此，可以不必花费太多力气，便能轻松地在其中一方面有所成果。从我研究无机药物的一点经验来看，这类工作给我带来巨大的满足感，无论是对研究者本人，还是为这个世界庞大的知识库增加了一点补充。回到实际情况，我们医学传教士在科学方面可以做些什么呢？

首先，详细记录我们所处站点的气象状况；至少要记录每日最高和最低气温，降雨量和降雪量，暴风雨或多云天气的日子，如果可以的话，记录下盛行风风向。这项工作不需要太多的仪器和时间，因此对学生或助手进行简单培训，便可每天定时记录观测结果。我有一本由华盛顿特区政府印刷局发行的《气象志愿观测者指南》。这本书可以通过给内政秘书写信申请从华盛顿免费获得。我从宾夕法尼亚州费州的 Messrs. Queen&Co 公司那里得到了气象仪器价目表。列表如下：

最高温度计：4.50 美元

最低温度计：3.50 美元

史密森标准温度计：5.00 美元

雨量观测器(镀锌铁):2.50 美元

因此,不到 20 美元,我们就能购买到上述符合观测要求的仪器。当然,如果我们想要更深入地研究这个问题,可能会花费更多的钱来购买额外的仪器,诸如气压计 30 美元、湿度计 6 美元、带有回旋装置的风速表 26 美元等等。

美国气象局欢迎志愿观察者的报告,我相信上述报告将会为其填补空白,且无需任何花费。不同站点的气象报告,结合当地流行病信息,必将帮助我们的董事会避免犯他们过去常犯的错误,比如将不合适的人派到不合适的站点,这不仅有损他们的健康,且徒劳无功。

其次,研究各地区的植物学。我很清楚,这项工作需要一些特殊的培训和专业技能,但至少,我们中有些人有能力在这方面做点什么。即使我们不能识别物种,但也应有足够的能力收集和制作标本,并将它们送到欧洲或美国的一些权威机构进行识别。

山东青州府(Chingchowfu, Shantung)的库寿龄(Couling)先生正在实践这一计划。他在其所在的地区收集植物,并把它们送到伦敦的英国皇家植物园(Kew Gardens)。他对寄出的标本作了详细的记录,以便在伦敦英国皇家植物园识别出这些标本时,他也能在这里辨认出他们。

第三,研究我们传教站的矿物学。任何在国内进行过化学特别是矿物学培训的人,都应该能够借助布拉什(Brush)矿物学分析系统来来确认我们在全国范围内所遇到的大部分岩石和矿物,也许还会增加当地地质学的知识。这是一个很容易在冬天进行的研究,尤其是在中国新年我们不太忙的这段时间。在我看来,我们这群人应该可以为这方面补充一些知识。

第四,研究当地的药物学。我们中有些人喜欢化学,并且在站点有实验室,他们很可能会花一点时间来研究本地商店的无机药物,尽管这可能是一个有点令人失望的领域,然而那些植物学家或药剂师却可以在中草药研究方面拥有非常广阔的空间。我想知道我们在 1890 年任命去调查当地药物学的委员会的调查进展。越与医学生接触,我越更加确信,我们应让他们熟知并充分利用当地可用的药物资源,这样在必要的时候,他们就可以自给自足,不需要依赖国外供给药物。他们中的许多人,在远离国外中心的地方行医，如果完全依赖国外获得的东西，他们的工作将很难继续。

以上仅仅列出几条建议，可以使在我们日常的医疗任务之外让自己感到高兴和满足。我们当然知道，我们的主要业务必须是照顾病人，并传播我们的救世主耶稣基督，尽可能供奉主和帮助中国人。同时，我感觉一个人除了他的主要事业之外，有一些爱好没什么不好，这对他来说也是一种休闲。我不认为我们的杂志会因此受到影响；相反，包含这些独立调查的记录会让杂志更有价值。

[摘自 *The China Medical Missionary Journal*, 1895, 9(3)]

Scientific Opportunities of Medical Missionaries

By James Boyd Neal, M. D.

Last autumn, as I went bumping along in a native cart on my way to our annual mission meeting at Wei Hien, a hundred and fifty miles from Chinanfu, and sat day after day looking out over the country, the thought came to me with great force what large opportunities we medical missionaries have for making and giving to the world scientific observations which would not only be interesting but really very valuable.

Our field in China is so wide and so little explored that it seems almost a virgin region with unlimited possibilities for investigation. There must be very few of us, scattered throughout the empire, who cannot snatch a little time from our regular daily duties to indulge in a little outside work in a scientific line. Then, too, many of us no doubt have had more or less special training in chemistry, mineralogy, geology, meteorology or botany, and could thus easily do a little work in one of these lines without very great extra labor. From a very slight experience in the line of investigating the native inorganic drugs I can testify to the great satisfaction which comes from such work, both to the man himself and from the hope that he may be adding some little to the world's stock of knowledge. But to be practical what could we medical missionaries do in a scientific line!

1st. Keep a careful record of the meteorology of the stations in which we are located; at least so far as to note the daily maximum and minimum temperature, amount of rainfall and snowfall and number of stormy or cloudy days, with, if possible, the direction of the prevailing winds. This work requires comparatively few instruments and very little time, as a student or helper can be easily trained to record the daily observations at certain fixed hours. I have before me a book of "Instructions for Voluntary Observers of the Signal Service", issued by the government printing office, Washington, D. C., which no doubt could be obtained from Washington free of charge by writing to the Secretary of the Interior and making request for it. A price list of meteorological instruments which I have from Messrs. Queen & Co., Philadelphia, Pa., gives the following:—

Maximum thermometer	Gold $4.50
Minimum thermometer	3.50
Smithsonian standard thermometer	5.00
Rain gauge, galvanized iron	2.50

So that less than twenty dollars in gold would be required to fit one out for making the observations outlined above. Of course if it is desired to go into the matter more deeply a large amount may be spent for additional instruments such as barometer $30, hygrometer $6, anemometer with whirling apparatus $26, etc.

The United States Signal Service welcomes reports from voluntary observers, and I believe will furnish blanks, free of charge, for sending in reports upon. Such reports upon the meteorology of our various stations, combined with some information in regard to prevailing diseases, would surely help to keep our Boards at home from making such blunders as they often do make in sending unsuitable men and women to unsuitable locations, to the great detriment of their health and usefulness.

2nd. Work up the Botany of our various Regions.—This, I am quite aware, requires some special training and some aptitude for such work, but surely some of us at least are capable of doing something in that line, and even if we cannot identify species might perhaps have skill enough to collect and press specimens and send them to some authority in Europe or America for identification.

Mr. Couling, of Chingchowfu, in Shantung, is following this plan, making collections of plants in his region and sending them to the Kew Gardens in London. He keeps a careful record of the specimens sent, so that when identified in London he may be able to recognize them here.

3rd. Study the Mineralogy of our Stations. —Anyone who has had practical training in chemistry at home, and especially in mineralogy, ought to be able with the help of Brush's System of Mineralogical Analysis to identify most of the rocks and minerals to be met in the course of our walks about the country, and perhaps might add much to the knowledge of local geology. This is a study which can so easily be carried on during the winter, and especially during the slack time at the Chinese New Year, that it seems to me we certainly ought to be able, as a body of men, to add something in this line to the general knowledge.

4th. Investigate the Native Materia Medical. —Those of us who are fond of chemistry and have a laboratory at our disposal may well spend a little time in a study of the resources of the native shops in the way of inorganic drugs, even though it may be a more or less disappointing field, while those who are botanists or pharmacists have a wide field open to them in the line of vegetable drugs. I wonder what has become of our committee which was appointed in 1890 to investigate the native material medical. The more I have to do with medical students the more I am convinced that we owe it to them to make them well acquainted with the native resources in the way of usable drugs, so they may be independent of the foreign supply in case of necessity. Many of them, practicing far away from foreign centers, will find it extremely hard to carry on their practice if solely dependent on what they can obtain from abroad.

The above are merely suggestions as to lines in which we might make ourselves useful and happy more or less aside from our regular medical duties. We all of course feel that our principal business must always be to minister to the sick and tell them of our blessed Savior Jesus Christ, striving in every way to please Him and help the Chinese. But in addition to this I cannot feel a man is any the worse for having a hobby apart from his main business which will be a recreation to him. Nor do I think our Journal will be any the weaker, but on the contrary far more valuable for containing records of such independent investigations.

1891～1896年
北美长老会济南医学工作报告

聂会东 著

济南府医疗工作

自1890年以来，没有发表一篇关于济南府(Chinanfu)医疗方面工作的报告。如今正是让在中国的同事们和在美国时刻关注着医院动态的朋友们了解一下过去6年中所进行的工作的时候了。过去的6年中，两所新医院建立，在美丽东郊的工作也正在稳步开展，这对济南府的医疗工作来说可以说是划时代的。

济南府的医疗工作是由洪士提凡医生(Dr. Stephen A. Hunter)在1879或1880年开始的，但直到1884年他才在市区主街道上的衙门前争取到了一块地皮，即便如此，获得的土地面积并不大，只有礼拜堂或药房那么大，建立医院是远远不够的。

在洪士提凡医生于1885年离职后，罗伯特医生(Robert Cultman, Jr.)接替了他的工作，直到笔者于1890年上任。从1891年11月到1893年10月，冯夏克医生(Dr. Van Schoick)会在我外出时负责工作的开展。

1880～1890年，人们一直坚持不懈地努力想得到一块地皮用来建立医院。直到1891年秋天，李佳白(Mr. Reid)先生成功地在东部城区的高地上——也就是如今文璧医院所处的区域，购买了一块土地。我们所做的工作获得了回报。1895年，我们在同区域购入了另外一块地皮，建立了一家女子医院，波因德克斯特医生(Dr. Sarah A. Poindexter)于同年4月在临时营地建立了药房和妇女儿童医院。

与此同时，日常配药在老城的药房中进行，在1893年前，药房的知名度是在不断上升的，但在那之后，由于主要的医疗工作被转移到东郊，以及受中日甲午战争和城市中新开业的西医药铺的影响，药房人数在不断减少，以至于在去年6月份我们不得不关闭了它。而从城市所处的状态考虑，这样的行动更是必须的——被荒废的城市已经不足以提供安全的治疗场所。

目前，在女子医院尚未开业的情况下，所有的医疗工作都是集中于郊区的文璧医院和女子药房。

大体的工作就阐述到这里。下表显示的是过去6年医疗工作中所有部门的数据。阅读此表后，我会分段阐述不同阶段的工作，并进一步介绍两家医院以及对医学生的教育培训。

表1　　整体数据

	1891年	1892年	1893年	1894年	1895年	1896年
文璧医院于1892年8月开业	…	1 839	6 015	5 033	5 738	10 721
女子医院于1895年4月开业	…	…	…	…	2 981	4 179
老城药房于1896年6月关闭	11 010	12 680	13 581	7 498	3 680	1 476
乡村地区病人	…	…	…	…	443	892
总　　计	11 010	14 519	19 596	12 531	12 842	17 268

6年总计患者人次为87 766。

文璧医院

该医院是依靠文璧先生(Rev. Jasper S. McIlvaine)的遗产建立起来的。文璧先生曾作为传教士在济南府及附近地区工作10年，他于1881年去世。地皮和建造医院的费用总计5 000墨西哥银元。在李佳白先生(Rev. Gilbert Reid)的监督下，主要用于配药的第一批建筑于1892年建立起来；同年8月份，在冯夏克医生的指导下，医院开始正式接收病人。

当笔者于1894年从北美归来时，全部建筑已在现址修葺完毕。

医院建造的平面图和建筑的形式完全是中国风格的。总共有三个院子，由南到北依次连接。首先是与正门入口相连接的门厅，两侧有两个为临时患者和贫困患者准备的房屋；其次是药房所在的庭院，两栋朝南的主建筑用于日常分配药物，侧面有两间屋子：一间是助手寓所，另一间是女子药房；最后是医院所在庭院，由一栋主楼和两边两栋建筑构成。医院中有三个大病房，各 12 英尺长、28 英尺宽，能够比较轻松地容纳 9 位病人。病房旁边有 3～4 个小房间，使医院总床位数达到了 35～40 个。然而，正如每位在中国北方有过医疗工作经历的人所知，这并不意味着医院在同一时间能够容纳这么多患者。由于医院不提供护士，所以患者无论在何种情况下必须有亲属或朋友陪同，这就意味着医院并不能容纳许多患者。到目前为止，最多有 20 位患者在同一时间接受治疗，因病房不足，其他的申请者被送到当地的小旅馆。

但是，必须要说的是，在医院的正后方，是与医院有着密切联系的医学生庭院，它最终将会成为医院的一部分，使总床位数达到 70 个。

自开业以来，医院相当受欢迎，在第一年中共有 6 000 余挂号人次。在中日甲午战争时期，每天来药房的人次有所下降，这使得 1894 和 1895 两年的总人数低于 1893 年。但在和平来临后，病人数量快速上升，该趋势一直持续到今天，使得去年的总挂号人数比前年增加了 5 000 人次，住院患者的数量也在逐年慢速稳步上升。

患者的特性

在多数情况下，被收入我们的教会医院的患者是来自农村地区的老年慢性病患者，他们想要在外国人开的诊所中待上几个星期以寻求病情缓解希望。在家庭医院中他们会被当作门诊患者，但在这里，若场地允许的话，我们并不反对将他们收入病房，这不仅是希望能帮助他们身体好转，更是为了能让他们有机会接受一段时间的宗教指导。

大部分患者来自遥远的地方，四五十英里的路程是非常普遍的，有时会有人走 150 英里来寻求治疗，也就是要花 4～5 天在路上。中国人非常有群体意识，以至于在很多情况下，一个到医院来寻求治疗的人会带来同乡的一大帮人。过去曾有一个接受白内障手术的患者，他来自 60 余英里外的村庄，竟有三四十个同乡人陪同他前来。病人需要自己提供寝具和食物，他们需要从餐厅中购买而不能在医院中做饭。所有的药物和治疗都是免费的，除了个别在药房内治疗的疾病以及有鸦片瘾的病人——他们需要在入院时缴纳 0.75 银元，以支付药物费用并确保他们能一直待到痊愈。我们曾尝试在城市药房向每位有支付能力的病人收取很少量的费用，但结果并不理想。我们相信，在纯粹的慈善工作中，收取费用并不会带来人们对基督教教义的好印象。

我们的大部分住院患者是来自周围地区的农民，但是药房中有来自各阶层的人们，既有衣着华丽的政府官员，也有邋遢的乞讨者。

每天早晨，医院的患者和医学生都会参加由值班的医师主持的祷告，下午则有福音传道者在门诊患者等候治疗时与他们交流，同时也向住院患者介绍教义问答手册和其他宗教用书。总体上来说，和我们共处了一段时间的患者看起来比较乐意了解和学习基督教。通过医院工作来直接增加教堂参与人数的成果并不显著，但也有几位满含希望的积极询问者，而与此同时，医疗工作也让人们对教会有了更为友善的印象，这一效果是毋庸置疑的。

治疗的疾病

一个有意思的现象是，连续 3 年中，医院治疗的眼科病例大概是住院人数的 1/3。这一数字远大于同时期的门诊患者的比例（门诊的比例只有 1/10）。

在过去 3 年的 490 位鸦片吸食者中，有 42 位成功戒掉鸦片瘾。

住院患者中，有 1/10 是来寻求肠胃病治疗的，包括消化不良、慢性胃炎、腹泻等。

在过去 3 年中，仅有 10 例间歇热和弛张热的案例，但这一数字并不能代表该地区疟疾的肆虐。去年夏天疟疾横行时，药房所接待的新病例中，1/4 都是疟疾患者。

在药房接触的病例中，除了上述的疟疾，其他流行疾病包括皮肤病、眼疾和肺病，其中慢性支气管炎和哮喘性支气管炎在冬季尤其普遍。肠胃疾病的案例也数量较大。下述表格给出了比前文更加细致的数据。在结束这个话题前，我希望能向一位忠诚而高效的医疗助手——马先生致敬。自 11

年前刚开始在山东省开始医疗工作时，他便是我的得力助手。找到我时他还只是一个配药师，之后他参加了第一期医学生班级并在所有的课程中名列前茅。毕业后他留在了济南府，年复一年，以忠诚尽责的态度履行着自己的使命。若文璧医院的工作取得了任何的成功，那这成就在很大程度上都归功于马先生的存在、对他人的影响和他自己尽职的工作。

表 2　　文璧医院数据

	1892 年	1893 年	1894 年	1895 年	1896 年
门诊患者新案例	966	2 930	2 250	2 430	4 613
门诊患者旧案例	850	2 964	2 648	3 158	5 903
住院病人	23	121	135	150	205
总　　计	1 839	6 015	5 033	5 738	10 721

表 3　　1894/1895/1896 年间文璧医院手术统计

	1894 年	1895 年	1896 年	三年总计
硬核性白内障	2	2	7	11
软性白内障	1	…	…	1
睑内翻和倒睫	21	11	20	52
眼球摘除术	1	…	…	1
虹膜切除术	2	…	…	2
翼状胬肉	11	9	11	31
睑球粘连	1	2	…	3
手指或脚趾截肢	1	2	3	6
包皮环割术	2	…	2	4
脱臼、骨折	1	2	…	3
肛管直肠瘘	3	5	8	16
碘注射治疗阴囊积水	2	1	…	3
石炭酸注射治疗痔疮	1	16	9	26
唇裂	…	3	1	4

续表

	1894 年	1895 年	1896 年	三年总计
鼻息肉摘除术	…	1	2	3
包皮切除	…	1	…	1
肿瘤、囊肿切除术	4	1	8	13
刺破脓肿等切开	76	46	58	180
拔牙	20	14	34	68
其他	8	9	1	18
总计	157	125	164	446

女子医疗工作

过去，女子医疗工作是与男子共同进行的，而在 1895 年 4 月，波因德克斯特医生为妇女儿童开了独立的医院和药房，此后，为了男女双方的便利以及增加妇女就医人数的目的，两个部门便一直分开。在波因德克斯特医生建立女子医院之前，有 3 000 余名妇女去过两个男子药房。在她工作开始后的八个半月时间中，波因德克斯特医生本人就问诊了数量如此之多的妇女患者，而在过去一年时间中，有 4 000 余人前来就诊。在 1895 年秋天和接下来的春天，一座造价 3 570 墨西哥银元的女子医院建立了。这是来自宾夕法尼亚哈里斯堡的波伊德女士(James Boyd)的馈赠。它有充足的门诊空间以容纳任何数量的患者；还有可接纳 20 余位住院患者的病房，病房采取的是传统的建筑方式，主楼朝南，以确保能在冬日获得充足的光照，在我们看来这一构造也能够最好地发挥医院的功能。对医院来讲不幸的是，波因德克斯特医生在建筑修建完成前与班特先生(Rev. Rufus H. Bent)完婚，并移居济宁州(Chining Chou)，使得新院的开业只能推迟到新的负责人到岗。

★女子医院

★学生庭院

目前，女子药房位于文璧医院的一栋建筑中，医疗助手马先生的夫人马女士除周日外，每天都会去接诊药房的病人，她曾受到波因德克斯特医生的训练，同时也师从她的丈夫。任何复杂的病症以及住院病例，都会受到笔者或他的助手的诊治。

当我前往芝罘时，波因德克斯特医生十分热心地从济宁赶来，在夏日中负责妇女医疗工作。她的热心肠令人十分感激，如果没有她的帮助我是不可能离开这个站点的。

医学生教育

系统的医学教育于10年前开始于登州府(Tengchowfu)，第一批5名男学生于1890年在济南结业。第二期课程立即启动，5名学生(包括一位中途去北京完成课业的学生)于1894年毕业。

10位毕业生中，有3位目前为教会工作，其余7位经营私人诊所。目前，第三期课程的5位学生学习进展稳步，他们的任务包括每周4～5天、每天2次的清晨背诵，每天下午则在药房帮忙。

课程是四年制的，学生们通过中文课本和日常背诵来学习化学和其他常规的医学科目，包括生理学、解剖学、药物学、治疗法、临床、外科手术、助产术、眼疾和皮肤疾病。

除了完成学位所需的4年学习外，学生们还被要求在教会医院或药房服务2～4年以充实他们的学习并且偿还一部分学费。每位男学生(除一位外)学习时每月会收到2墨西哥银元，而毕业后他们每月会得到5～7墨西哥银元。在过去的几年中，我们为课程需求准备了眼科疾病、皮肤疾病、治疗法和解剖化学方面的教科书。眼科和化学的课本已经出版，皮肤疾病的课本大概今年会出版。从事医疗教育的同僚们可能会感兴趣的是，我们在山东尝试了合作式的医学教育。第二期的学生们在济南用一年半的时间跟我学习了化学、解剖和生理学后，去沂州府(IChowfu)用一年半的时间向章嘉礼医生(Johnson)学习临床和外科手术。

回到济南后，学生们再用一年的时间结束学业。目前的课程也是遵循同样的计划，但是由于章嘉礼医生的助手们离开了他，学生们不得不在向章嘉礼医生学习了几个月后便回到济南。我认为这一教学模式十分有利，这给了学生们看到不同的疗法、听到不同的讲解的机会，尤其是当传教站之间相距不远时。在第二期课程中，该教学模式的效果十分令人满意。

聂会东于文璧医院

1897 年 1 月 6 日

[备注:感谢帕奇先生(Rev. Virgil F. Partch)提供的各建筑的照片]

Chinan Fu Medical Work

No report of this work having been published since the end of 1890, it seems fitting that fellow-workers in China and friends in America, who are interested in the hospitals here, should be told of what has been done during the past six years. This is more especially so because these few years have marked an era in the medical work in Chinan Fu, two new hospitals having been built, and the work established on a seemingly firm basis in the open ground of the east suburb, among healthful surroundings.

Medical work was begun in Chinan Fu by Dr. Stephen A. Hunter in 1879 or 1880, but it was not until 1884 that he secured a suitable permanent location on the main street of the city, in front of the prefect's yamen, and even then the premises obtained were large enough only for street chapel and dispensary, no hospital accommodations being afforded.

When Dr. Hunter left the station in 1885 his place was taken by Dr. Robert Coltman, Jr., who continued in charge until in 1890, when the writer of this report came. From December, 1891, until October, 1893, Dr. I. L. Van Schoick had temporary charge of the work during my absence on furlough.

During all the years from 1880 to 1890 efforts were being constantly made to secure a location for a hospital, but without avail until the autumn of 1891, when Mr. Reid succeeded in purchasing a piece of land, well located on high ground in the east suburb, on part of which the present McIlvaine Hospital was soon afterwards erected. In 1895 another piece of ground was secured in the same region and a new Women's Hospital built, Dr. Sarah A. Poindexter having opened a dispensary and hospital for women and children in temporary quarters in April of that year.

Meantime daily dispensing was carried on at the old city dispensary, which up to 1893 continued to steadily grow in popularity. Since that year, owing no doubt partly to the fact that the main medical work had been moved to the suburb, partly to the effect of the Japanese war, and partly because several foreign medicine shops have been opened up in the city, the attendance had decreased to such an extent that it was deemed wise to close the place last June. Such action was, moreover, rendered almost a necessity by the state of the city premises, which were becoming so dilapidated as to be unsafe for occupancy.

At present the medical work is all centered in the suburb in the McIlvaine Hospital and Woman's Dispensary, the hospital for women not having yet been opened.

So much for a general view of the situation. The table below gives the statistics of all departments of the medical work for the past six years. After giving this it may be interesting to take up the different phases separately and give some further account of the two hospitals and of the training of medical students.

General Statistics

	1891	1892	1893	1894	1895	1896
McIlvaine Hospital opened Aug, 1892	…	1,839	6,015	5,033	5,738	10,721
Women's Hospital opened April, 1895	…	…	…	…	2,981	4,179
Ctiy Dispensary closed June, 1896	11,010	12,680	13,581	7,498	3,680	1,476
Patients seen in the country	…	…	…	…	443	892
Totals	11,010	14,519	19,596	12,531	12,842	17,268

Total attendance for six years 87,766

McIlvaine Hospital

This hospital was built with part of the proceeds of a legacy left by the

Rev. Jasper S. McIlvaine, who for ten years was a missionary in Chinanfu and vicinity, and who died here in 1881. The total cost of land and buildings amounted to about $5,000 Mexicans. The first buildings, mainly for dispensary purposes, were erected in 1892, under the supervision of Rev. Gilbert Reid, and the premises were opened for the reception of patients in August of that year by Dr. Van Schoick.

On the writer's return from America the buildings were completed in 1894, as they at present stand.

The plan and general architecture are entirely in Chinese style. There are three courts in all directly succeeding each other from south to north, namely, a gate court into which opens the main entrance, and in which are two small side houses for transient and the poorer class of patients; next a dispensary court with large main building, facing south, used for daily dispensing, and two side houses, one of which is the assistant's dwelling, and the other at present is occupied by the Women's Dispensary; and lastly a hospital court with one main and two side buildings. In the hospital proper are three large wards, 12 × 28 feet each, capable of accommodating, without crowding, nine patients a piece. Besides these wards there are three or four smaller rooms, making the capacity of the hospital from thirty-five to forty. As every one knows, however, who has had any experience in hospital work in North-China, this does not mean that this number of patients can be accommodated at any one time. Owing to the number of friends and relatives who come with patients, and who are really necessary in any serious case, as the hospital does not furnish nurses, a considerably smaller number fills the premises. Up to the present only about twenty patients have been under treatment at any one time, any additional applicants being sent to native inns' for lack of room.

It should be said, however, that directly behind the hospital, and in intimate connection with it, is a court for medical students, which will eventually become part of the hospital, thereby increasing its capacity to about seventy.

The hospital has been fairly popular from the time of its first opening, some six thousand attendances having been registered during its first full year. During the time of the Japanese war there was a falling off in the daily visits at the dispensary, so that the total numbers for 1894 and 1895 do not equal the total of 1893; but soon after the conclusion of peace there began to be a marked increase in attendance, which has continued to the present, making the total for the past year nearly five thousand larger than for the year preceding. The number of in-patients has been growing from year to year with a slow but steady increase.

Character of Patients

The patients received into our mission hospitals in the interior are, in many cases, old chronic sufferers who come up from the country to spend a few weeks on the foreign premises in hope of relief. In home hospitals they would be treated as out-patients, but here, when there is room to accommodate them, we are not averse to taking them in, not only in the hope of being able to help them physically, but also for the sake of giving them the opportunity of being under religious instruction for a time.

The patients often come from long distances for treatment, a journey of forty or fifty miles being a very common occurrence, and at times they come as much as a hundred and fifty miles, a four or five days' journey. The Chinese are so clannish that not infrequently one man's coming to the hospital and receiving benefit will be the means of bringing a crowd from his neighborhood. One man during the past year, from a village sixty odd miles away, operated upon for cataract, has attracted some thirty or forty people to the hospital from his region. Patients are required to furnish their own bedding and food, which as a rule they are expected to buy from restaurants, not to cook themselves on the premises. All medicine and treatment are free, with the exception of certain diseases treated in the dispensary and of the opium habit patients, who are required to pay $0.75 on entrance, to cover the cost of medicines and to further ensure their remaining until cured. We tried charging a small entrance fee to all patients able to pay at the city dispensary, but it did not seem to work well. We have not yet been convinced that the charging of fees in what is supposed to be a purely benevolent work, is calculated to produce a favorable impression for Christianity.

The majority of our in-patients are farmers from the surrounding districts, but the dispensary practice brings representatives from all classes, from the well-dressed official to the filthy beggar.

Religious Instruction

Morning prayers are held every day with the hospital patients and medical students, led by the physician in charge, and in the afternoon an evangelist talks with the dispensary patients while awaiting their turn for treatment, and also instructs the in-patients in the catechism and other religious books. Generally those patients who stay with us for some time, seem glad to listen to instruction and to study Christian books. The direct results from the hospital work in the way of addition to church membership have not been large, but there are several who seem to be very hopeful inquirers, while the general effect of the medical work in creating a better feeling towards the work of the church is apparent and markedly good.

Diseases Treated

It is an interesting fact that for three successive years the number of eye cases treated in hospital has been about one third the total number of in-patients. This is a much larger proportion than prevails among out-patients, among whom during the same period only about one-tenth have been eye patients.

Of patients treated for cure of the opium habit there have been forty-two during the past three years out of a total of 490.

About one-tenth of the hospital patients have been under treatment for gastro-intestinal troubles, such as dyspepsia, chronic gastritis, diarrhea, etc.

There have been but ten cases of intermittent and remittent fever treated in hospital during these three years. This, however, by no means represents the frequency of malarial diseases in this region. During the malarious months of the past summer nearly one-fourth of the new cases at the dispensary were malarial patients.

In our dispensary practice, aside from the malarial troubles just referred to, the prevailing diseases are those of the skin, eye and lungs, chronic bronchitis and asthmatic bronchitis being especially widespread during the winter months. Gastrointestinal troubles are also numerous. Below will be found more detailed statistics of the work of the hospital than those given in the beginning of the report. Before closing the subject, however, I should like to bear testimony to the faithfulness and efficiency of the medical assistant, Mr. Ma, who has been my right hand man ever since begin-

McIlvaine Hospital Statistics

	1892	1893	1894	1895	1896
Out patients—New Cases…	966	2,930	2,250	2,430	4,613
„ „ Old „ …	850	2,964	2,648	3,158	5,903
Hospital Patients … …	23	121	135	150	205
Total …	1,839	6,015	5,033	5,738	10,721

List of Operations in McIlvaine Hospital, 1894-95-96

	1894	1895	1896	Total 3 years
Eye Operations:—				
Cataract, Hard … …	2	2	7	11
Soft … … …	1	…	…	1
Entropium and Trichiasis …	21	11	20	52
Enucleation of Eye-ball …	1	…	…	1
Iridectomy … … …	2	…	…	2
Pterygium … … …	11	9	11	31
Symblepharon …	1	2	…	3
Amputation of Finger or Toe …	1	2	13	6
Circumcision … … …	2	…	12	4
Dislocations and Fractures set	1	2	…	3
Fistula in Ano … … …	3	5	8	16
Hydrocele in jected with Iodine	2	1	…	3
Hemorrhoids injected with Carbolic Acid … … …	1	16	9	26
Harelip … … … …	…	3	1	4
Nasal Polypi extracted … …	…	1	2	3
Prepuce amputated … …	…	1	…	1
Tumors and Cysts removed	4	1	8	13
Abscesses,etc,lanced … …	76	46	58	180
Teeth extracted … … …	20	14	34	68
Miscellaneous … … … …	8	9	1	18
Totals …	157	125	164	446

ning practice in Shantung eleven years ago. Coming to me at first as a mere dispenser he joined the earliest class of medical students and took highest rank in his studies all through his course. Since graduating he has continued in Chinan Fu, performing his duties from year to year in a most faithful and conscientious manner. If the work of the McIlvaine Hospital is in any measure a success it is due in large part to the presence, influence and faithful work of Mr. Ma.

Medical work for Women

The work for women was formerly carried on in connection with that for men, but in April, 1895, Dr. Sarah A. Poindexter opened a separate hospital and dispensary for women and children, and since that time the two departments have been kept separate, to the manifest advantage of both and with the result of perceptibly increasing the attendance of women. During the year preceding the opening of Dr. Poindexter's hospital there had been somewhat over three thousand women seen at the two men's dispensaries. In the first eight and a half months of her service nearly as many were seen by Dr. Poindexter alone, and during the past year over four thousand visits have been registered. In the autumn of 1895 and the following spring a new hospital for women was built, costing about $3,570 Mexicans. This was the gift of Mrs. James Boyd, of Harrisburg, Pennsylvania. It has ample accommodations for the seeing of any number of out-patients; and room for twenty or more in-patients is built in native style with main building facing south, so as to secure the maximum amount of sunlight in winter, and will, we think, prove suitable and convenient for the purpose for which it is intended. Unfortunately for the hospital Dr. Poindexter was married to Rev. Rufus H. Bent before the completion of the building, and has since removed to Chining Chou, so that the opening of the same has been postponed until some one else comes to take up the women's work.

At present the women's dispensary occupies one of the buildings belonging to the McIlvaine Hospital, the dispensary patients being seen every day, but Sunday, by Mrs. Ma, the wife of the medical assistant. She has been partially trained by Dr. Poindexter during her stay here, and more or less taught by her husband. Any difficult cases and those received into hospital, are seen by the writer or his assistant.

During my absence in Chefoo, Mrs. Bent very kindly came up from Chi-ning Chou and took charge of the women's work through the summer months, a kindness which was most highly appreciated, as otherwise it would have been impossible to have left the station.

Training of Medical Students

Systematic teaching of medicine was begun ten years ago in Teng-chow Fu, and the first class of five young men finished the course in Chinan Fu in 1890. A second class was started immediately, and five more (including one who went to Peking to finish his studies) graduated in 1894.

Of these ten three are in mission employ and seven are in private practice. At present there is a third class of five studying regularly. Their work consists of two recitations each morning, four or five days in the week, and they also assist each afternoon in the dispensary.

The length of the course is four years, during which time they go over chemistry in addition to the regular medical studies in physiology, anatomy, material medical and therapeutics, practice, surgery, obstetrics, eye diseases and skin diseases, all of which they study by means of textbooks in Chinese and by regular recitations.

In addition to the four years required for graduation they are expected to spend from two to four years in some mission hospital and dispensary in order to supplement their regular course and to repay, in a measure, the cost of educating them. Each boy, with one exception, receives about $2 Mexican per moon, while studying. After graduating they command fromfive to seven dollars per Chinese month. During the past few years textbooks have been prepared for the use of the classes in eye diseases, skin diseases, therapeutics and analytical chemistry. Those on the eye and on chemistry are already published, that on skin diseases will probably be published during the present year. It may be of interest to those engaged in medical instruction to know that we have tried the plan of co-operative teaching of medicine in Shantung. The second class of students after spending a year and a half in Chinan Fu, finishing with me chemistry, anatomy and physiology, went to Ichowfu for a year and a half's study with Dr. Johnson, who took them over most of practice and surgery.

On their return here they spent a year finishing up their course. The present class started in to pursue the same plan, but owing to Dr. Johnson's assistants leaving him they were compelled to return to Chinan Fu after only a couple of months with Dr. Johnson. I am inclined to think favorably of such a plan, especially if mission stations are not too far apart, as giving students an opportunity to see different methods and hear varied instruction. The result in the case of the second class was very satisfactory.

James Boyd Neal, M. D.
McIlvaine Hospital,
January 6th, 1897.

(P. S.—The report is indebted to Rev. Virgil F. Partch for the pictures, which he has kindly furnished of the various buildings.)

中国医学教育的现状

聂会东 著

1896 年下半年，作者给在中国各地医学差会发出约 140 份问卷，调查他们所在地区的医学教育状况。我们已经收到反馈回来的 60 份问卷，其中 21 份问卷报告他们所在地区没有进行定期的教学。另外 39 份问卷数据汇总见下表，呈现了他们所在地区医学教学的现状和迄今已完成的工作。首先，最令人鼓舞的是我们资深的嘉约翰博士(Dr. Kerr)和他的同事们在广州(Canton)训练年轻男女医学生方面所取得的卓越成就。嘉约翰博士说，广州的教学工作始于 1835 至 1840 年间，当然因为这些记录不完整，因此表中的数字为大约的数字，总共培训了 100 人以上。虽然数据不完整，但从问卷中的数据，我们看到在广州的博医会医院已经通过受过系统西方医学教育的医生帮助了中国人，给他们提供卫生服务，培养的学生人数是其他医院的 4 倍。

其次，需要引起大家注意的一点是教学的班级规模很小；只有包括香港在内的 5 个教学点，每个班有超过 10 名学生，而绝大多数地区的班级只有 2～6 名学生。这似乎表明在大多数情况下，即使在注册的医学生中，教学也主要是让学生跟随主管医生日复一日地或多或少断断续续地学习并阅读医学书籍，并没有任何规律和系统的教学。换句话说，在中国真正能称得上医学学校的不足 6 个。在这方面，应当指出的是，目前为止还没有收到上海方面的任何回复，据作者所知，那里并没有进行任何医学教学。当你想到作为中国中心的上海拥有许多设施齐全的医院却没有进行任何医学教育，这就显得非常奇怪了，因为在人们的心目中会想当然地认为那里应该有一个先进的医学教育中心。

我们非常高兴地发现有几个地区正在积极推进女医学生的培训；尤其是在福州(Foochow)，那里的马斯特兹博士(Dr. Masters)有一个 9 名学生的医学班，戈达德博士(Dr. Goddard)的医学班有6名学生，他们的班级里都有女医学生。在福州和广州，女性似乎成了医学班级不可缺少的组成部分。

我认为所收到的这些回复给人的总体印象是有些失望，到目前为止只完成了如此少的工作，但同时我们也对未来抱有希望。

中国人接受西方医学教育的兴趣明显快速增长，随着兴趣的增长我们可以寻找更好的方法，开办更大规模的班级，进行更集中更高效的工作。现在看来，缺少接受过基础课程教育的年轻学员是阻碍医学教育进步的巨大障碍，基础课程教育对成功的医学教育是必不可少的。在山东，我们并不缺乏申请者，但是当经过一年的筛选，我们淘汰掉那些无法跟上的学生后，课堂通常从14或15人减少到5～6人。这个难题当然只能通过在我们教会学校和学院的稳步增长的毕业生来解决，或者我们愿意培养更加年轻的学生并教育他们完成物理学、化学等初级课程的学习，为医学课程的学习做准备。然而后者，在大部分开展医学教育的地区是行不通的；现在的情况是很难有充足的时间完成已经开展的医学教育。作者希望在这本杂志中刊登这次的调查反馈就是期望能够引起大家对从培养学生的最好方法到使用的教材、需要开设的课程等的全面讨论。然而我们或许会感到欣慰的是，当前有250～300名学生和助手，他们或多或少在各医院里接受过西医教育，并且现在约有300人受雇于私人诊所或医院，我认为我们应该致力于招收更多的学生和开展更深入、更系统的教学。

医学培训班。广东(Canton)、杭州(Hangchow)、济南府(Chinanfu)和奉天(Moukden)的医学培训工作开展得相对较好。梅藤更博士(Dr. Main)认为医学培训工作很重要，因为外国人不能独立完成所有的工作，普通的本地医生又是"一群江湖医生"。聂会东博士的班上有5名学生，他们每天完成2次课程温习，每个下午在药房帮忙。这些学生，跟随聂会东博士学习一段时间以后，就被送到另一个工作站，跟随章嘉礼博士继续其他课程的学习。这种合作教学法受到聂会东博士的高度评价，认为它是目前解决医学生培养问题的有效途径。

医学培训班统计表

所在地	医师	受训总数	教会雇佣人数	私人执业人数	在校男生数	在校女生数	在校生和毕业生总数	在校年限
广州	Dr. Kerr	79	不详	不详	18	6	103	3 或 4
天津总督医院	Houston				26		26	
苏州	Park	9	5	3	10	6	25	5
杭州	Main	12	7	5	8	3	23	5
香港	Thomson	7		7	12		19	5
福州	Whitney	14	2	10	3		17	5
青州府	Masters	16	8	5 *	无	无	16	
福州	Watson	6	2	4		9	15	6
沈阳	Christie	9	2	7	6		15	5
济南府	Neal	10	3	7	5		15	4
北京	Curtiss	4	2	2	9		13	4
保定府	Atterhury	13		13	无	无	13	
福州	Goddard	4‡	无	无		6	10	6
南京	Stuart	4	1	2ξ	5		9	5
漳州	Fahmy	3		3	6		9	5
重庆	MeCartney	3	3		5		8	5
孝感	Otte	4		4	4		8	5
金华	Barchet	2	1	1	4		6	5
汕头	Scott	3	3		3		6	4
潮州府	Cousland				4		4	5
永春	Cross				4		4	5
平度	Randle				3	1	4	4
锦州	Brander	1		1	2	1	4	4
成都	Kilborn				3		3	4
其他	15 地	65	22	41	21	1	87	
		268	61	115	161	33	462	

注：* 3名去世； ‡ 全部去世； ξ 1名去世； + 沂州府的章嘉礼医生(Dr. Johnson)，协助一个班5名学生的培训。

[摘自 *The China Medical Missional Journal*. 1887,11(2)]

Medical Teaching in China

By James Boyd Neal, M. D.

In the latter part of 1896 about one hundred and forty circulars were sent out by the writer to the various medical missionaries in China, asking for information in regard to the status of medical teaching in the stations where they were located. To these circulars sixty replies have been received, of which twenty-one report no regular teaching carried on. From the remaining thirty-nine answers the following table, showing the present state of medical teaching and what has so far been accomplished, has been compiled. The first point perhaps which strikes one in glancing over the table, is the preeminent position held by our veteran, Dr. Kerr, and his colleagues in Canton in the training of young men and women in medicine. The work of teaching in Canton was begun between 1835 and 1840, and the records are necessarily incomplete, so that the figures in the table are only approximate, more than one hundred in all, according to Dr. Kerr, having been trained. But with all its incompleteness, and taking the figures as found in the table, we see the Medical Missionary Society's Hospital in Canton has helped the Chinese, in the way of furnishing them with physicians trained in foreign methods, four times as much as any other hospital in China.

The next point to be noted is the smallness of the classes taught; there being only five places in all China, including Hongkong, where there is a class of more than ten students, the vast majority consisting of from two to six only. This would seem to indicate that in most instances, even where medical students are reported, the teaching consists in allowing the students to pick up what they can in daily association with the physician in charge and from more or less desultory reading of medical books, without any very regular and systematic teaching. In other words, that scarcely half a dozen places in China have arrived at the point where they can be really considered to be medical schools. In this connection it is to be noted that no replies have been received from Shanghai, and so far as the writer knows no medical teaching is being carried on there. This seems the more strange when one thinks of the numerous and well-equipped hospitals in Shanghai and of its commanding position as the very center of China, where one would naturally expect to see a strong central medical school.

It is gratifying to find that in several places the training of women in medicine is being pushed; especially is this so in Foochow, where Dr. Masters has a class of nine, and Dr. Goddard, a class of six. At Foochow and Canton too the women seem to form an integral part of the medical classes.

The general impression made by the returns I think is one of disappointment that so little has been accomplished so far, and yet at the same time of hopefulness for the future.

Interest in the training of the Chinese in Western medicine is evidently increasing rapidly among the physicians in China, and as that interest develops we may look for better methods, larger classes, and altogether more efficient work. The one great difficulty which seems to block the rapid advance of medical teaching is the scarcity of young men and women who have had the preliminary training necessary to the successful study of medicine. We in Shantung have no lack of applicants, but when after a year's sifting we eliminate those who are not able to keep up, we find our classes usually reduced from fourteen or fifteen to five or six. This difficulty of course can only be overcome by the steady growth in the numbers educated in our mission schools and colleges, or by our being willing to take our medical students at younger age and put them through a preliminary course of physics, chemistry, etc., preparatory to medicine. This latter plan, however, would be quite impracticable in most places where medical teaching is carried on; the difficulty now being to find the time necessary to do the teaching of even the ordinary medical studies. It is the hope of the writer that the publication of these returns may lead to a full discussion in the pages of the Journal of the best methods to pursue, books to be used, length of course to be required, etc., in the training of our students. While we may feel gratified that there are today probably two hundred and fifty or three hundred students and assistants who are becoming more or less thoroughly trained in Western medicine in our various hospitals, and perhaps three hundred now in private practice, we should, I think, aim at much larger numbers and more thorough systematic teaching.

Medical Training Classes. —At Canton, Hangchow, Chinanfu, and Moukden special attention is given to this branch of work. Dr. Main considers this work all important, as foreigners cannot do all the work that needs to be done, and as the ordinary native doctors are such a "pack of quacks and impostors". Dr. Neal has a class of five students, who have two recitations daily and assist each afternoon in the dispensary. These students, after spending a time under Dr. Ncal, are sent to another station, where under Dr. Johnson they pursue a course of study on other subjects. This co-operative method of teaching is highly spoken of by Dr. Neal, who thinks it the solution of the problem of teaching medical students.

Location	*Phyician*	*Total number trainea.*	*Number in Mission Emplay.*	*Number in Prioute Practice.*	*Men now in training.*	*Women now in training.*	*Total Number already trained and now in training.*	*Years required.*
Canton …	Dr. Kerr — …	79	Not kown	Not kown	18	6	103	3or4
Tientsin-Viceroy's Hospital	,, Houston …	…	…	…	26	…	26	…
Soochow …	,, Park … …	9	5	3	10	6	25	5
Hangchow …	,, Main … …	12	7	5	8	3	23	5
Hongkong …	,, Thomson …	7	…	7	12	…	19	5
Foochow …	,, Whitney …	14	2	10	3	…	17	5
Chingchowfu	,, Watson … …	16	8	5*	None	None	16	…
Foochow …	,, Masters … …	6	2	4	…	9	15	6
Moukden …	,, Christie … …	9	2	7	6	…	15	5
+Chinanfu …	,, Neal … …	10	3	7	5	…	15	4
Peking …	,, Curtiss … …	4	2	2	9	…	13	4
Paotingfu …	,, Atterhury …	13	…	13	None	None	13	…
Foochow …	,, Goddard …	4‡	None	None	…	6	10	6
Nanking …	,, Stuart … …	4	1	2§	5	…	9	5
Changchow …	,, Fahmy … …	3	…	3	6	…	9	5
Chungking …	,, MeCartney …	3	3	…	5	…	8	5
Sioke… …	,, Otte … …	4	…	4	4	…	8	5
Kinhwa …	,, Barchet … …	2	1	1	4	…	6	5
Kakchieh …	,, Seott … …	3	3	…	3	…	6	4
Ch'aochowfu	,, Cousland …	…	…	…	4	…	4	5
Eng-chhun …	,, Cross … …	…	…	…	4	…	4	5
Pingtu …	,, Randle … …	…	…	…	3	1	4	4
Chinchow …	,, Brander … …	1	…	1	2	1	4	4
Chentu …	,, Kilborn … …	…	…	…	3	…	3	4
Miscellaneous	15 places in all …	65	22	41	21	1	87	…
		268	61	115	161	33	462	

* Three dead.

Dr. Johnson, of Ichowfu, assisted in the training of one class of five students.

‡ All dead.

§ One dead.

文璧医院(一)

聂会东 著

文璧牧师(Rer. Jasper S. McIlvaine)于1881年他去世之前在济南府的主要街道上购买了一处房产,打算让当地的教会用作建立教堂、诊所和会议的场所。但是文璧先生在得到房产之前就去世了,之后人们发现很难以和平的方式获取他所购买的房产,最后被换成了一处较小的地方,我们将其用作教堂和诊所。除了这处小房产之外,文璧先生的遗产还包括一笔可观的资金。

在与文璧先生的直系亲属协商后,决定将这笔钱留在济南府传教站使用。首先用于建立一所医院,其次是建造一座教堂供教会使用。一年年过去了,人们一直在努力寻找一个合适的地方,直到1891年,文璧先生去世10年后,终于在城市东郊的开阔地买到了一块理想的地方。

1892年春天,第一批建筑终于建成,包括宽敞的门诊、助手的房子和用来收治劳动阶层病人的普通病房,还有一些必要的附属建筑。1892年8月,冯夏克医生(Dr. Van Schoick)开始在新建筑中开展医疗工作,自那以后医疗工作步入正轨。在1898年,医院收治了近6 000名门诊患者和100多位住院患者,其中包括在医院接受治疗的瘾君子。1893年秋至1894年春,医院在主建筑基础上扩建,在诊所后面又建造了三幢独立房屋,可以容纳25～30名住院患者。1894年6月这些建筑完工并准备投入使用,至此,文璧医院已经完工,并建立了一座纪念碑,以纪念这位仁爱热忱的差会先驱。

医院大约可容纳40名住院病人和数不清的门诊患者。这些建筑都采用中式风格,建有三面围墙和一个开阔的庭院,建筑总共有3个院子,分别是门庭、药房和医院。

用其他资金建造的培养医学生的建筑，位于医院后面，能够容纳 12～14 名年轻人。目前，12 名年轻人刚刚开始在医院接受为期 4 年的定期学习，致力于成为西医执业医师。

负责医院工作的人，无论是本地助手还是外国人，他们不仅缓解病人身体上的痛苦，而且带领病人认识基督教。如果文璧先生能够回来，一定会对他的遗产的使用感到非常欣慰。传教站目前仍有相当可观的资金，他们正在寻找其他合适的地方用于建造教堂。

（摘自 *The Church at Home and Aboard Relating to China and Chinese*，1894-1896. Vol. 4）

The McIlvaine Hospital

By James Boyd Neal, M. D.

Rev. Jasper S. McIlvaine, some time before his death in 1881, had purchased a valuable property on the main street of the city of Chinanfu, intending the same for the use of the native church as a chapel, dispensary and general meeting place. Before possession was obtained of the place Mr. McIlvaine died, and it being found impossible to gain peaceable occupation of the property which he purchased, it was exchanged for a much smaller location, which is at present used as a street chapel and dispensary. We received, in addition to the property, a considerable sum of money.

After consultation with Mr. McIlvaine's immediate family, it was decided to use the money thus left in the hands of the Chinanfu Station, first in the erection of a hospital, and second, in helping to build a chapel for the use of the native church. As time went on, efforts were constantly made to effect the purchase of a suitable site, but it was not until 1891, more than ten years after the death of Mr. McIlvaine, that land was finally secured in a most desirable location in open ground in the east suburb of the city.

Here, in the spring of 1892, the first buildings were erected, consisting of a large and commodious dispensary for use in treating daily patients, houses for assistants, and a couple of inferior wards for the accommodation of the less desirable class of patients, besides necessary outbuildings. Medical work was begun in the new buildings by Dr. Van Schoick in August, 1892, and has been carried on regularly ever since, there having been an attendance at the dispensary during 1898 of nearly six thousand, besides over one hundred in-patients, including opium smokers treated in the hospital. During the autumn of 1893, and the spring of 1894, work was pushed upon the main court of the hospital, consisting of three separate and detached buildings placed immediately behind the dispensary, and capable of accommodating twenty-five or thirty patients. These buildings were completed and ready for occupancy in June, 1894, so that now the McIlvaine Hospital is complete, and stands a noble monument to the memory of a loving and earnest pioneer in missionary work.

The capacity of the hospital is about forty in-patients and an indefinite number of dispensary patients. The buildings are all in native Chinese style, built about the three sides of open court yards, there being three court yards in all—Gate Court, Dispensary Court and Hospital Court.

Just back of the hospital and directly connected with it, though built with entirely separate funds, are buildings for the training of medical students, capable of accommodating a class of twelve or fourteen. At present, twelve young men are just beginning a regular four years' course of study in the hospital, with a view to becoming practitioners of medicine according to western ideas.

In as much as the aim of those in charge of the work of the hospital, both native assistants and foreigners, is to make it the means not only of relieving physical distress, but of leading the patients to a knowledge of Christ, we can not but feel that Mr. McIlvaine, if he could return, would not be displeased with the disposition which has been made of his legacy. There still remains a considerable sum of money in the hands of the station treasurer to be applied toward the erection of a chapel when additional suitable ground can be obtained.

文璧医院(二)

聂会东 著

文璧牧师(Rer. Jasper S. McIlvaine)1881 年在济南府去世,他是山东西部新教差会的创始人和长老会济南站的创建者。他是一个虔诚的、真正热爱中国的人,他留下了大约 5 000 美金的遗产供济南府的教堂使用,证明了他对这个国家和人民的热忱。但是多年来一直买不到合适的建筑和土地,大部分的资金在这 10 年间放在银行里产生利息,只有一小部分被用来在这座城市的主要街道边上建造了一所小教堂和药房,成为多年来基督教工作的中心。

在 1891 年,在东郊高地上一块合适的土地被买了下来,在这里文璧先生的钱大部分被投资在一所有 40 张床位的医院上,这所医院为了纪念他被命名为文璧医院;纪念牌位被放在围墙里最显眼的地方,用英语和汉语向人们介绍文璧先生和这所医院是怎样建造起来的。我们把大部分的遗产投入医院而不是其他事业,是因为从文璧先生到达济南府直到能够购买土地的今天,这所城市仍然仇视外国人,我们认为最好是在新地点马上正式开始正规医疗工作(药房的工作已经开展了很多年),希望以此感化人民。

正规的医疗工作于 1892 年 8 月在新医院开始,我们希望用慈善工作吸引人们的注意力,现实也并没有让我们失望。在 1893 年,也是医院工作的第一个整年,共有 6 000 多人前来就诊,其中 121 名患者住院治疗。在接下来的两年里,由于中国和日本之间的战争(注:甲午战争),这一数字多少有所下降,但在 1896 年就诊人数超过 10 000 人次,1897 年是我们能够找到完整记录的最后一年,之后所有的书籍都在义和团运动中遭到损毁,当年就诊人数超过 11 000 人次,其中有 260 住院病人。尽管缺少女医生,如果 1897 年的数据也包括女性患者,她们也去文璧医院看病,那么总数将接近 16 000 人,表明医院在创建后的 5 年中医疗工作呈现出非常可喜的发展。

1900 年的义和团运动给医院造成了严重的打击，至今还没有完全恢复。所有的工作记录，从 1897 到 1900 年都被摧毁了，医院关闭了约 1 年，经过全面维修和改建，在 1901 年 6 月重新开放。值得庆幸的一点是，在动乱期间，由于所有的建筑物都是中式风格，它们得以幸免，只有仪器和药品被洗劫一空，这样的损失是可以承受的，因此 1901 年差会成员返回后重开医院并不困难。自医院重新开放以来的 3 年中，工作一直稳步进行，而且每一年就诊人数都有所增长，尽管就诊人数还没有达到往年的数字。在 1902 年共有约7 000人次；1903 年约 8 000 人次，其中包括近 150 例住院病人，而今年看起来将有约 10 000 人次。当然这些数字只统计了男性患者，妇女和儿童患者在另一个医院接受我们的女医生伯汉姆博士(Dr. Mary L. Burnham)的治疗。

在过去的 3 年里，我们在济南府的医疗工作中最令人欣慰的是已经实现收支平衡，无需因医院的运作向外国差会寻求资金。每一年捐款簿都在济南府的中国官员中传阅，从知府开始，他捐赠了 100 土耳其里拉(Turkish Lira)，大大小小的官员和富裕的病人还有其他中国朋友紧跟其后，最后还有外国的支持。这些捐款满足了我们的大部分需要，另外我们要求那些有能力的患者支付他们的药费，我们也从销售奎宁、鱼肝油等药品中得到了相当可观的收入。全部的这些收入已经足够用来支付我们运行所需的费用。

不要忘记我们现在在西部郊区有一个由政府支持的有竞争力的对手。但不管怎样，我们都应对文璧医院的未来和它在济南府的工作充满希望。

(摘自 *China Medical Missionary Journal*, 1905, Vol. XIX)

McIlvaine Hospital, Chinanfu.

By James Boyd Neal, M. D.

In 1881 there died in Chinanfu the Rev. Jasper S. McIlvaine, who was the pioneer of Protestant missions in Western Shantung and the founder of the Chinanfu Station of the Presbyterian Board. A man of eminent piety and of real love to the Chinese, he testified to his interest in the people by leaving a legacy at his death of about $5,000 in gold for the use of the Chinese church in Chinanfu. As, however, it was impossible to procure suitable buildings or to buy land for some years, most of this fund lay at interest in bank for ten years, only a small part of it being used to fit up a street chapel and dispensary on the main street of the city, which was the center of Christian work for many years.

In 1891 land was procured in a most desirable location on high ground in the east suburb, and here most of Mr. McIlvaine's money was invested in a hospital with accommodations for forty patients, which has been named in his honor the McIlvaine Hospital; memorial tablets being erected in prominent places inside the walls, telling in English and Chinese who Mr. McIlvaine was and how the hospital came to be built. The reason for putting most of the legacy into a hospital rather than any other form of work, was that from the time that Mr. McIlvaine arrived in Chinanfu up to the time that we were able to purchase land, this city was noted for its hostility to foreigners, and it was thought best to start regular hospital work (dispensary work had been going on for many years) as quickly as possible on our new site, in the hope of conciliating the people.

Regular medical work was begun in the new buildings in August, 1892, and we were not disappointed in our hope of drawing the people to us by our philanthropic work, as during 1893, the first full year of the working of the hospital, there were six thousand attendances in all, including 121 patients treated in hospital. During the two years following there was a slight falling off in numbers, owing to the war between China and Japan, but in 1896 there was a total attendance of over ten thousand, and in 1897, the last year that we have full records of until after the time of the Boxer troubles, when all the books were destroyed, there was a total attendance of over eleven thousand, including 260 hospital patients. If in the figures of 1897 are included the women patients, who were also seen in the McIlvaine Mcltvaine Hospital, Chinanfu. Hospital in the absence of the lady doctor, the total amounts to nearly 16,000, showing a very gratifying development of the medical work during the five years of its existence.

The Boxer disturbances in 1900 dealt the hospital a very severe blow, from which it has not yet fully recovered. All the records of the work from 1897 up to the year just mentioned, were destroyed, and the hospital was closed for about a year, being reopened after extensive repairs and alterations in June, 1901. It was a matter of great congratulation that during those troublous times the buildings, all of which are built in Chinese style, were not destroyed; only instruments and drugs being looted, so that the loss sustained was of moderate amount and did not hinder the reopening of the hospital after the return of the members of the Mission in 1901. During the three years since the reopening, the work has been carried on steadily and has been growing moderately year by year, though the total attendance has not yet reached the numbers recorded in previous years. In 1902 there were about seven thousand total attendances, about eight thousand in 1903, including nearly 150 in-patients, while this current year will show about ten thousand; these numbers applying only to men; the women and children being treated in a separate hospital, which is under the care of our lady doctor, Dr. Mary L. Burnham.

The most interesting development in connection with our medical work in Chinanfu during the past three years is the attainment of self-support; no funds being now asked from the Board of Foreign Missions for the running of our hospitals. Every year a subscription book is circulated among the Chinese officials in Chinanfu, beginning with the governor, who starts the list with a contribution of Tls. 100, and is followed by all the other officials of any considerable rank in the city among the well-to-do patients and other Chinese friends, and finally among foreign supporters. From these contributions we receive the bulk of what we need, but in addition we ask those among the patients who are able to, to pay for their medicines and have also a considerable income from sales of quinine, cod liver oil, etc.; the total amount received being sufficient for all our running expenses.

Taking it all in all, and remembering that we now have a rival hospital supported by the governor in the west suburb, there is reason to look forward hopefully to the future of the McIlvaine Hospital and its work in Chinanfu.

中国博医会

聂会东 著

约 20 年前，也就是 1886 年，经过文恒理博士(Dr. Boone)和其他一些关注此问题的人的不懈努力，中国的医学差会经投票成立了博医会，并出版了相关领域的杂志。

博医会成立的章程第二条中写道，该协会成立的目的是：

第一，促进西医在中国的推广，以及促进来自国内医学传教士的相互交流和帮助。

第二，促进传教工作和西医的进步。

第三，通过维持信仰的和谐与统一，促进协会成员的特质、兴趣与荣誉感。

杂志第一期于 1887 年 3 月出版，杂志的头篇文章就是文恒理博士写的关于这个新成立协会未来工作的设想。这里，我想引用其中的一段话，这些话虽然写于 20 年前，但依然适用于现今。文恒理博士在文章中写到：

中国的医学传教士应该感谢这伟大的事业，近来的选举使他们团结一心。我们现在有条件为共同的目标而努力，以前所未有的机会认识和欣赏彼此。我们的联盟会给我们团队精神，缺乏这种精神，我们将不能团结一致，我们的努力也将成为一盘散沙。我们的季刊《医学杂志》首次为我们建立了一个平台，报告我们的工作，并逐步总结、积累有益于人类和世界的观察和经验。我们是能够向世界证明所做工作值得尊重与支持，还是由于怠慢疏忽而失去了出版杂志的机会，都取决于我们自己。

参考了杂志中的一系列问题，其中一部分将在博医会的会议上详细讨论。文恒理博士提出了如下我们需要深入思考的问题，这个问题也会是本次会议的中心议题:怎样才能获得周围中国人的尊敬并影响他们,引导他们获得更加深入的思考和生活。

对照博医会成立的宗旨和文恒理博士文章中所着力论述的问题,试问我们协会在何种程度上完成了它建立的目标?对于我们今后几年工作的改进有什么建议?

首先,我们为"促进西医在中国的推广"这个目标做了些什么?

如果这条章程仅是指在中国上下建立药房和医院的话,那么我认为我们可以公正地说,这个目标在过去的18年里已经如期完成。我们的治疗中心分散在这片土地的各个地方,虽然很多地方仍未被开拓,但我们仍然可以感到自豪,因为每年都有成百上千的人在我们的药房和医院里得到救助,我们每年都会在新的地点开展医疗服务。即使是在1900年那灾难性的一年,实现目标的动力也促使我们建造更好的建筑和在动乱的地区增加医疗工作。任何熟悉中国医疗事业发展的人都会知道,尽管尚有许多工作要做,我们在过去的15年中取得的进步是明显且鼓舞人心的。

如果"促进西医在中国的推广"这个目标是指建立正规医学学校、系统进行医学教育并培养医学人才的话,恐怕我们就要承认自己的失败了。在统计过去一年杂志收集的医疗数据时,笔者很惊讶地发现在中国几乎所有的医疗中心都在尝试开展医学教学。现在,虽然我们应该对零星的年轻人正在接受西医教育感到高兴,并且他们正在准备比本地的赤脚医生做得更好,但我们必须承认的事实是:在普通医院中,无法获得足够的时间和精力来培养医学生。多年的个人经验及差强人意的经历告诉我,这种培训充其量只是一种权宜之计。如果我们有受过系统医疗训练的本地医学人才,我们一定会让这些人在中央医学院校中奉献自己最大的能量,而不是让他们在日常医疗工作之外再用剩余的精力进行教学。但这样的学校在中国有多少?这个协会,无论是总会还是当地的分支机构,是否支持筹建过哪怕一所这样的学校?恐怕没有。然而,时代的信号正在变得更加明显。预计在北京(Peking)、济南府(Chinanfu)或漳州府(Changchowfu)、汉口(Hankow)建立的三座联合医学院看似有很好的发展前景。同时，众所周知，这样的学校已在广州落成，并有望为中国的南部带来巨大的好处。迟早，每个省会都应该有这样一个医学教学中心，到时候，大家都要全身心投入，帮助联合办学取得巨大成功。同时，作为一个协会，我们是否可以在任何可行的地方鼓励组建这样的联合学校？

第二，我们做到了多少工作来促进这个国家不同的差会之间相互交流经验？

就我个人而言，我在医学协会的经验中得到了很大的帮助和鼓励，也经常在杂志上发表我的经验，对我来说，这本杂志当然值得出版。但从长期观察和作为该杂志编辑 3 年以来的经验看，我不得不承认，我们作为一个团体，并没有通过发布"多种经验"而达到互相协助的目的。正如文恒理博士所言，"我们是能够向世界证明所做工作值得尊重与支持，还是由于怠慢疏忽而失去了出版杂志的机会，都取决于我们自己。"我认为我们恐怕需要承认我们没有任何手段将我们在医院和药房里哪怕一半的工作展示给人们，暂且不表我们为自己和世人收集的关于中国的生活状况的知识。但事实是该杂志的编辑收集的信息甚至没有得到一半以上医院的回复，尽管我们再三要求这样做，这显示了我们当中的一部分人有非常令人失望的不团结行为。考虑到每个人都要忙于自己的日常工作，原始调查数据的缺乏虽然并不特别令人惊讶，但这仍然很让人遗憾。在中国之外的医生也需要我们的启示，因为这些问题只有居住和调查过这里的人才能解决。更令人失望的是，除了医学，我们也没有在气象学、植物学以及大家普遍感兴趣的其他学科作出更多报道。

自从在杂志上通过"互相帮助"的协议，我们作为一个协会，上次相聚已经是 15 年前了，难道不是一个遗憾吗？我相信我们很多人深感遗憾，并衷心希望我们以后会有一个 3 年一次的会议，以便经常切磋，面对面地接收从事相同神圣工作的同事们的灵感。这样频繁的会议似乎更令人向往，因为在许多情况下，医务人员不可能很长时间离开他们的岗位，如果我们经常开会，协会的所有成员都有希望能偶尔出席。

第三，到目前为止，作为章程的第二部分，如上面所述，我认为我们在传教工作方面已经相当成功，作为舆论共识是：医疗工作是传教工作直接有力的帮助，和十分卓越的开辟新土地的手段。

没有人可以说我们应该做的已经都做完了，而且在许多情况下，毫无疑问，我们觉得还没有充分利用好医学在传播福音方面的作用，不管是作为医务人员的我们，还是我们的文职同事。作为直接教导福音的场所，为了赢得人心，医院病房就是一个很好的开端，但如果想要收获果实，则必须在病人离开医院后进行后期跟进，恐怕在这一领域我们并没有得到应有的收获。

第四，关于“在这个国家维持信仰的团结与和谐”，协会已经起了很大作用。我们高兴地发现近几年来来到中国的人都很急切地加入协会，所以我们的会员已将大多数在中国的工作人员包括在内。但仍有很多能够获得会员资格的人需要我们将之招收入内，我特别建议邀请更多地海关人员和私人执业医师成为会员。这样的话无疑会增强我们的影响力，使我们更多地接触到出色的阶层。我应该说，我们的协会应该包括国内每一个受人尊敬的医生。会员人数的加强意味着力量的加强，不仅是因为数量的增加，而且还有更多的对杂志的贡献和收入，这些都可以使杂志更好。

我简单地叙述了在过去几年中我们所完成的和未完成的事，现在该考虑一下我们未来的计划了。考虑到可能会有些人持不同想法，我谨提出以下几点未来几年建议：

1. 把所有在中国的医学传教士，甚至日本和韩国的医学传教士都纳入医学传教士协会，同时尽可能多地把与我们目标一致的私人行医者纳入协会。

2. 将我们的《医学杂志》改为双月刊，我们当中的每个人尽自己所能每1～2年在杂志上发表一篇文章，来使我们的杂志建立在更加扎实的基础上。如果每个人每年至少写一篇文章的话，那我们的杂志就可以做成月刊了。

3. 创立一本中文的医学杂志来为我们越来越多的医学毕业生使用。

4. 在基督教的影响下，尽我们所能，在中国更多的重要城市建立中央联合医学院。

5. 采取措施，出版系统统一的中文医学科学丛书，采用协会在此次会议上通过的新医学名词。

6. 采取行动，在我们的医学教学和医学教科书中引入公制单位。

[摘自 *China Medical Missionary*, 1905, 19(1)]

The Medical Missionarv Association of China

James Boyd Neal, M. D.

It was in 1886, nearly twenty years ago, that through the efforts of Dr. Boone and others, who were particularly interested in the matter, a vote was secured from the medical missionaries then in China favoring the formation of an Association and the publishing of a journal in its interests.

The Constitution in Article Ⅱ says. —

The objects of the Association shall be—

First. —The promotion of the science of medicine amongst the Chinese, and mutual assistance derived from the varied experiences of medical missionaries in this country.

Second. —The cultivation and advancement of mission work and of the science of medicine in general.

Third. —The promotion of the character, interest, and honor of the fraternity by maintaining a union and harmony of the regular profession in this country.

The first number of the JOURNAL was published in March, 1887, and the first article in that number was by Dr. Boone on the future work of the newly-formed Association. From that article I may be permitted to quote a few sentences, which are just as applicable now as they were when written, nearly a score of years ago. Dr. Boone says:-

The medical missionaries of China have great cause for thankfulness that, by the recent election they have been brought into common bonds of union and sympathy. We are now in a condition to work together for the common good, to know and appreciate one another in a way we never have had a chance to do before. Our union will give us that esprit du corps, without which we can never do good work as a body, and our best efforts would be scattered and unsupported. In our quarterly MEDICAL JOURNAL we have now, for the first time, an organ in which to express ourselves, to report upon our work, and to enable us to garner the constantly increasing mass of observations and experience for the good of our own body and of the world in general. It rests with us whether we shall show the world that we are doing work which will command respect and support, or whether, by our own spineless, we lose the opportunity which the publication of this JOURNAL places at our disposal.

After referring to a number of questions for discussion in the JOURNAL, some of which will come up for consideration during these meetings, the doctor asks the following heart-searching question, which might well be made the central thought of the present conference:

What have you found to be the best method of gaining the respect, the attention and the power to influence the Chinese around you, so that you say lead them to higher thinking and living than they have ever had any opportunity of attempting before.

With these few quotations from the constitution and from Dr. Boone's article as an introduction, may we not profitably ask ourselves how far our Association has accomplished the objects for which it was founded? And what improvements can we suggest for the coming years?

First. —What have we accomplished for the "promotion of the science of medicine amongst the Chinese"?

If this section of the constitution refers merely to the establishment of dispensaries and hospitals throughout the empire, then I think we may fairly say that this object has been accomplished as far as could reasonably be expected during the eighteen years' life of the Association. Our centers for healing are scattered over the length and breadth of the land, and while we have to acknowledge that an immense amount of territory still remains unoccupied, yet we may point with pride to the hundreds of thousands who every year obtain relief in our scores of dispensaries and hospitals and to the new places which are being opened up from year to year. Even the troubles of 1900, which for the time being were so disastrous, have resulted in finer buildings and in increased medical work in the disturbed districts. To anyone at all well acquainted with the development of medical work in China, the advances made during the past fifteen years are quite marked and very encouraging, even though so much does still remain to be done.

But in so far as "the promotion of the science of medicine amongst the Chinese" depends upon the establishment of regular medical schools and the careful training of medical men by means of systematic instruction, I fear we shall have to acknowledge that we have largely failed. In compiling the statistics of medical work sent in to the JOURNAL during the past year, the writer was much struck with the fact that nearly every medical center in China was attempting to do medical teaching. Now, while we cannot but be glad that these scattered groups of young men are being taught something about rational medicine, and are being prepared to be something better than the native quacks, yet we all recognize the fact that it is impossible to give the requisite time and attention to the training of medical students in connection with our ordinary hospitals. Such training is a makeshift at best, as the writer well knows from years of personal and rather unsatisfactory experience. If we are to have native medical men trained as thoroughly and carefully as they should be trained, we are bound to have central medical schools with men in them who are set apart to devote their best energies to this work and not expected to do medical teaching merely as a side issue with the remnant of strength left after attending to their regular practice. Yet how many such schools have we in China? And has the Association, either in general or by its local branches, endorsed a single one? I fear not. The signs of the times, however, are brightening. There seems a good prospect of a union medical school in Peking, another in Chinanfu or Changchowfu, and a third in Hankow, while, as is well known, such a school has been already inaugurated in Canton, and bids fair to be a great boon to the southern part of the empire. Sooner or later every provincial capital should be supplied with such a center of medical teaching, and when the time comes let us all put our shoulders to the wheel and help to make such union schools a grand success. Meantime can we not, as an Association, encourage the formation of such union schools wherever it is practicable?

Second. —How far have we enjoyed mutual assistance from the varied experiences of medical missionaries in this country?

Personally I feel that I have derived great help and encouragement from the experiences of my medical associates, as published from time to time in the JOURNAL, and to me the JOURNAL has always seemed well worth publishing. But from long observation of its career and from a three years' experience as editor of the JOURNAL, I am forced to concede that we, as a body, fail to do what we could very easily do to mutually assist each other by publishing our "varied experiences". As Dr. Boone so well says, it has rested with us to show the world that we are doing work which will command respect and support, or by our own spineless lose the opportunity which the publication of this JOURNAL places at our disposal. I fear we shall have to acknowledge that we have not by any means shown the world half of what is being accomplished from year to year in our hospitals and dispensaries, and that we have not added, as we should have done, to our own and the world's stock of knowledge of the conditions of life in China. The very fact that it has been impossible for the editors of the

JOURNAL to obtain full returns (or even meagre ones) from more than half the hospitals in China, notwithstanding repeated requests for the same, shows a spineless on the part of some of us which is very disappointing. There has been a dearth too of original investigation on the part of us all, which, while not particularly surprising, considering the fact that each one has his own daily work to look after, is nevertheless to be regretted. Physicians outside of China have a right to expect us, who are on the ground, to enlighten them as to problems which can be solved only by residence and investigation in this country. Aside from purely medical questions I have been disappointed that we have not reported more on the meteorology and the flora of China, as well as other subjects of general interest.

Passing from the question of mutual aid through the pages of the JOURNAL, does it not seem a pity that it should be fifteen years since last we met together as a general Association? I am sure many of us feel it to be so, and heartily wish that we might hereafter have a meeting once in three years, so as to oftener compare notes, look into one another's faces and receive the inspiration of numbers engaged in the same blessed work. Such frequent meetings seem all the more desirable, because in many cases it is impossible for medical men to get away from their posts except at long intervals, and if we had meetings frequently there would be more hope of all the members of the Association being able to be present occasionally.

Third—So far as the second section of the Constitution, quoted above, is concerned, I think we may say that we have succeeded fairly well in the "cultivation and advancement of mission work", as the general consensus of opinion seems to be that the medical work is a most valuable adjunct to direct missionary effort, and as a means of opening new territory is quite unsurpassed.

None of us can claim that all has been done that might have been done, and in many cases no doubt we feel that not nearly the use has been made of the medical work as an evangelistic agency that might have been made,—either by us medical men ourselves or by our clerical colleagues. As a field for the direct teaching of the Gospel, and for winning one's way to the hearts of people, the wards of our hospitals are certainly a grand place to begin, but to reap the fruits of such efforts they must be followed up after the patients leave the hospital, and I fear that here is where we fail to get out of our medical work the spiritual results which we have a right to expect.

Fourth. —As to "maintaining the union and harmony of the regular Profession in this country", the Association has filled a useful place, and it is gratifying to find that those who have come to China during recent years have seemed anxious to join the Association, so that the membership now includes the large majority of those practicing in China. Much, however, still remains to be done in the line of enrolling all who are eligible for membership on the books of the Association, and especially would I suggest the advisability of inviting more of the Customs and other medical men in private practice in China to become members. Such a course will undoubtedly strengthen our influence and bring us more in touch with a class of men many of whom are doing excellent work. Our Association ought, I should say, to include every respectable man who is practicing medicine in China. Such an increase in membership means increased power, not only through the weight of numbers, but also in the greater variety of contributions to the JOURNAL and the increased income which will be available for making the JOURNAL better.

Having thus briefly sketched what we have accomplished, and what we have left undone, during the past years, it may be profitable to consider what should be our plans for the future. With all due deference to the opinions of those who may think differently, may I suggest the following as some of the objects we should accomplish during the next few years.

1st. —Enroll all medical missionaries in China, and Possibly Korea and Japan, in the Medical Missionary Association, and as many private practitioners as are in sympathy with our aims.

2nd. —Establish our MEDICAL JOURNAL on a more solid basis by making it a bi-monthly and by determining that each one of us will do all in his or her power to make it a success by writing for it at least once in every year or two. The JOURNAL could easily be made a monthly if every one would write only one article a year for it.

3rd. —Establish a medical journal in Chinese for the use of our increasing number of medical graduates.

4th. —Throw all our influence in favor of the establishment of central union medical schools, under Christian influences, in the more important cities of the empire.

5th. —Take measures looking to the issue of a uniform series of textbooks of the medical sciences in good Chinese, in accordance with the new nomenclature to be passed upon by the Association at this Conference.

6th. —Take action favoring the introduction of the metric system in our medical teaching and in our medical textbooks.

中国目前的现状

聂会东 著

在中国的历史上，从来没有像现在这样对商业和基督教传教如此开放。特别是义和团运动以来，政府态度的改变令人不可思议。对于在这个国家生活了多年的我们来说，之前这个国家的大门一直紧紧关闭，而现在大门敞开，我们被邀请自由进入，这简直难以置信。

我清晰地记得，在我来到济南的第一个10年中，我唯一一次被允许进入政府衙门的经历。根据李鸿章的建议，我应邀看望山东省省长，并将他的病情汇报到天津(Tientsin)，这样李鸿章就可以派自己的私人医生照顾他。去衙门那天是在一个星期天的下午，我发现省长肩上有一个巨大的疮，报告了天津，回复说不要做进一步的处理。周四，李鸿章的私人医生欧文(Irwin)来到这里，但是省长已经接近临终，他只能暂时缓解病人的痛苦，也别无他法。省长当天晚上去世了，随后谣言四起，说外国医生把他毒害死了，还提到这与我上个周日去拜访省长也有关系。于是有告示贴出要驱逐这个城市的所有外国人。有段日子我们很担心群众暴动，但是政府注意到这件事情，把这些违规的告示撕下，几天后，事情平息了。

这是1891年发生的事情，自那以后的10年间，据我所知没有外国医生进过政府衙门。1901年，义和团运动之后我们返回到这里。韩维廉先生(Hamilton)、莫约翰先生(Murray)和我以私人名义去拜访袁世凯以感谢他在那段艰难的日子里给予山东传教士的帮助。随后不久，他的母亲身患疾病，他让我多次前去诊治，每次他都对我表现出自然简单的关心以及他对他母亲健康的关切。

袁世凯在山东任巡抚时没有召开过任何大的招待会，他的继任者也是如此。但是当周馥(现任南京总督)来到山东时，在不同的场合举办很多招待活动，在那里外国人有机会遇见省里所有的高级官员。如果不是他举办的这些宴会，并时常邀请外国传教士，任何有声望的外国人都不可能有机会拜访政府官员。周馥在任时举办的这些宴会让外国人和本地人之间相互有了很好的了解，没有什么比这更好的了。

他不仅在公共场合表达对外国人的友好，私下里他也让我和其他医生为他开处方，每年都捐款支持我们的医学工作。

★郭显德的助手

周馥的继任者杨士骧省长，一年前来到济南府，继续举办前任所开办的宴会，在 11 月 6 号，慈禧太后生日那天，他举办宴会邀请所有在济南府的外国人，包括男士和女士。我们不仅有幸见到所有的官员，更令人高兴的是看到洋溢在中国人、外国人之间的友谊，这与几年前的情况形成了鲜明的对比。

上面显示出现在外国人和中国人间的友好关系，而在这之前，双方处于敌对的状态。而且除此之外，有种种证据都表明了中国态度越来越开放：如建立一所花费超过 $150 000，有 300～400 名学生的省级学院；开办有 300 名学生的师范学校；不仅在山东省会济南府，而且还在山东省的其他城市建立的农业大学和军事学院以及许多不同等级的学校等。不仅是在山东的省会济南，在其他城市也是如此。其他省份也愿意接受国外先进技术，他们希望自己适应 20 世纪开放年代的变化。每个地区都对发展教育、开发国家自然资源、在中心城市修建铁路表现出很大兴趣。所有的一切都显示了利用好当前开放的政策是何等重要，我们应通过各种手段，加强在中国的传教工作。

[摘自 *Presbyterian Magazine*, 1906, 12(1)]

Some Phases of The Present Situation in China

James Boyd Neal, M. D.

Never in the history of the Empire has China been so open to not only business enterprises, but also to the preaching of the Gospel as at this present moment. The change which has taken place in the attitude of the officials, especially since the dreadful days of the Boxer trouble, has been simply marvelous. To us who have been in the country for a good many years it seems almost incredible that doors which many years were so stubbornly shut against us should now be wide open, and we be invited to enter freely.

Well do I remember, the only time that I was allowed to enter the walls of the Governor's yamen in Chinanfu during the first ten years of my location here. At the suggestion of Li Hung-chang I was invited to go to see the Governor of Shantung and report upon his condition to Tientsin, so that Li might send down his own private physician to attend him. It was on a Sunday afternoon that I went to the yamen. I found the Governor suffering from a huge carbuncle on his shoulder and so reported by telegraph to Tientsin, not being allowed to do anything further. On Thursday Li Hung-chang's private physician Dr. Irwin, arrived but found he could do nothing for the patient but give him something to relieve his pain, as he was then nearing his end. The Governor died that night and immediately the rumor was spread abroad that he had been poisoned by the foreign doctor, and as my visit on the previous Sunday was also mentioned in connection with the matter, placards were put up about the city urging the driving out of all foreigners. For some days we were in considerable fear of mob violence but the officials were vigilant and had the offending placards torn down and in a few days the affair quieted down.

This was in 1891. From that time until ten years later so far as I know, no foreign physician was inside the Governor's yamen. In 1901, on our return after the Boxer trouble. Messrs. Hamilton, Murray and I went to call in person on our then Governor Yuan Shihkai to thank him for all his kindness to the missionaries in Shantung during those terrible times, and were received by him most cordially. Not long afterwards his mother was taken ill and he had me go to see her several times, each time showing himself most simple and unaffected in his bearing toward me as well as in his solicitude for the welfare of his mother.

Yuan Shih-kai himself never gave any large entertainments while in office in Shantung, nor did his immediate successor, but when Governor Chou Fu, who is now Viceroy in Nanking, came to Shantung, he began giving really very delightful entertainments on various occasions, at which the foreigners in town had the opportunity of meeting all the highest officials in the Province. No foreigner of any prominence could visit Chinanfu without having such a feast given in his honor, and to these feasts the members of the missionary community were not infrequently invited Nothing could have contributed more directly to a kindly understanding between foreigners and natives than such pleasant gatherings as Chou Fu gave during his term of office.

Not only did he show himself thus friendly to foreigners in a public way, but in private he constantly called in not only myself but other physicians to prescribe for him, and contributed regularly every year to the support of our medical work.

Chou Fu's successor, Governor Yang, who came to Chinanfu about a year ago, is continuing the public feasts inaugurated by his predecessor. Only today (November 6th), on the occasion of the birthday of the Empress Dowager, he gave an entertainment and reception to which all the foreigners in the city were invited, including both ladies and gentlemen. While rather a mixed affair it was nevertheless pleasant to meet all the officials and see the spirit of friendliness which prevails between foreigners and Chinese, in such vivid contrast with the state of affairs in former days.

The above will serve to show what cordial relations now exist, in this formerly hostile city, between foreigners and Chinese in a social way. Besides this, however, the evidences of advance are manifest on every side in the establishment of a Provincial College of between three and four hundred students, on which over $150,000 have been expended; the opening of a Normal School with three hundred scholars; the establishment of an Agricultural College and Military College, and in the opening of numerous schools of various grades, not only in Chinanfu, the provincial capital, but also in many other cities of the province. Nor is Shantung peculiar in this respect. Other provinces are probably quite as advanced in this adoption of foreign ways, and their wish to adapt themselves to the changed conditions of these opening years of the twentieth century. Everywhere there is manifest the greatest interest in the development of education and the exploiting of natural resources of the country and the building of railways with Chinese capital. All which shows how important it is to take advantage of the present open door and strengthen by every means our missionary forces in China.

济南的联合医科大学

聂会东 著

20 多年来，山东医学生的培养由各地医生和不同的差会进行；有时是由一个医生或者差会，有时是由两个或三个一同进行。然而，这样的培训方式一直被认为是远远不能令人满意的；由于缺乏实验设施，学生未能得到足够的基础培训，也未能在更加注重实践的内科和外科获得适当的训练。

所以在 1902 年，山东规模最大的差会团体——英国浸礼会和美国长老会建议成立教育工作联盟时，在联合教育委员会中工作的唯一一位医生立即提议这个联盟应该在设有文理学院与神学学院的同时还应包括一所医学院。这一点得到了委员会其余大多数成员的赞同，得到了差会和国外舆论的赞同，因此，从本省联盟运动开始之初，我们就一直在考虑建立一所联合医科大学。

然而，不幸的是，我们既没有适当的可立即使用的场所，也没有足够的人手能够离开自己的传教点，集中在某个中心地区工作，并把全部时间用于培训学生。所以，我们决定不在寻求这样的合作培训中浪费时间，而是马上开始我们所谓的“流动”课程。因此，在过去的 5 年里——这也是自从联盟实际上开始运行的 5 年，在获得场地、建筑和宿舍前，联合医学课程已经由上述两个团体的医务人员开展起来。去年我们在济南府南部郊区获得了一块土地，是这一城市发展最迅速的地方，学校现在正在建设过程中，我们有信心能够在 1910 年 3 月 1 日前完工。三层的主楼将有足够的解剖学、生理学、组织学和病理学教室和实验室，还将提供药物学和实用药学深入研究的专门设施。现代化设施的医院将为医学生进行内科和外科实习提供便利。

整个建筑是由伦敦浸礼会提供的，由艾宗敦(Arthington)基金赞助，虽然建筑物属于英国浸礼会，如前所述，学院是一个联合机构，处于英国浸礼会和美国长老会的共同管理下，通过大学理事会，医学院成为山东大学一部分。我们自信地期待山东其他的新教团体，甚至一些临近的省份，将参与到这个联盟中为中国培养基督教医生。

学院的课程持续6年；第一年在潍县(Wei Hien)联合学院学习物理、化学、生物学、植物学；其余的5年将在济南学习医学专业知识。学生须达到20岁(中国传统计龄)才能入学，必须支付5墨西哥元的半年度费用，每年总共10元，还有食物、书籍等费用。我们认为每年50元即可支付全部费用，包括学费、食品、书籍和旅行费用。

所有的教学都是中文的。目前，医学院师资队伍由下列外籍人员组成，由具备能力的中方人员协助：

韦特恩医生(Dr. E. Freiherr von Werthern)，

武成献医生(Dr. James Russell Watson)，

巴德顺医生(Dr. Thomas C. Paterson)，

章嘉礼医生(Dr. Charles F. Johnson)，

聂会东医生(Dr. James Boyd Neal)

上述名单中的章嘉礼，韦特恩和聂会东博士将会在学院中定期任教，而武成献和巴德顺博士将在他们其他职责允许时到学院授课。除此之外教师队伍已经安排妥当，我们期望隶属于临近机构的其他医务工作者，能够到学院给学生授课。

如果有人对上述机构有兴趣，可以从笔者处获得英语和中文的简介。

(附图)

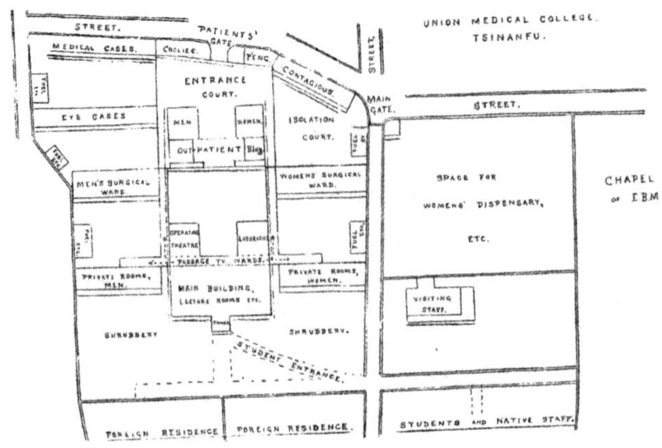

Frout Elevation of Main Building.
UNION MEDICAL. SCHOOL., TSIXAXFU.

[摘自 *China Medical Missionary Journal*, 1909, 5(9)]

The Union Medical College in Tsinan

James Boyd Neal, M. D.

For over twenty years the training of medical students has been carried on in Shantung by various physicians and by different missions; sometimes by one individual alone, sometimes by a combination of two or three. It has always been felt, however, that such training was far from satisfactory; the pupils failing to get the training in the foundation branches which they should have, owing to lack of laboratory facilities, and also failing to receive the proper drill in the more practical branches of medicine and surgery.

When therefore it was proposed in 1902 to establish a union in educational work between the English Baptist and American Presbyterian Missions, the two missions having the largest work in Shantung, it was immediately suggested by the only medical man on the Joint Educational Committee that this union be made to include a Union Medical College, as well as a College of Arts and Science and a Theological College. This was most readily agreed to by the other members of the committee and endorsed by the missions and the home societies, so that from the very beginning of the movement for union in this province the idea of establishing a Union Medical College has been in our minds.

Unfortunately, however, no proper premises were immediately available, nor was it possible to assign men to the work who could leave their own stations and live in some central place and devote their whole time to training students. Nevertheless it was determined not to lose any time in securing cooperation in such training, but begin at once to work together in carrying on what we called "peripatetic" classes. Accordingly during the past five years—that is ever since the union actually went into effect—

union medical classes have been carried on by the medical men of the two missions concerned, pending the obtaining of a site and the erection of buildings for the accommodation of the union college. Such a site was secured last year in the south suburb of Tsinan, in the most rapidly growing section of the city, and buildings are now in course of construction, which it is confidently expected will be ready for occupancy by the first of March, 1910. The main three-storied building will provide ample accommodations for lecture rooms and laboratories for the practical study of anatomy, physiology, histology, and pathology. Special facilities will also be provided for a thorough study of material medical and practical pharmacy. A modern equipped hospital will give facilities for the practical instruction of the medical students in clinical medicine and surgery.

The whole plant is being provided by the Baptist Missionary Society of London, from grants made by the trustees of the Arthington Fund, but while the buildings belong to the English Baptist Mission, the college is a union institution, as stated above, under the joint control of the English Baptist and American Presbyterian Missions, through the medium of the University Council, the college being the medical department of the Shantung University. It is confidently anticipated that other Protestant missions in Shantung, and possibly in some of the adjoining provinces, will share in this union undertaking for the training of Christian doctors for China.

The course continues through six years; the first being occupied with the study of physics, chemistry, biology, and botany in the Union College in Wei Hien; the last five being devoted to purely professional studies in Tsinan. Students must be 20 years old (Chinese) on entrance, and must pay a semi-annual fee of five Mexicans, ten dollars in all per year, besides providing their own food, books, etc. It is thought that fifty dollars a year will probably cover the total cost, including fees, food, books, and travel.

All teaching will be in Chinese. The teaching staff of the Medical College, so far as at present constituted, consists of the following foreign members, who will be assisted by competent Chinese:—

E. Freiherr von Werthern

James Russell Watson

Thomas C. Paterson

Charles F. Johnson

James Boyd Neal

Of the above named Drs. Johnson, von Werthern, and Neal will teach regularly in the institution, while Drs. Watson and Paterson will give such courses of instruction as their other duties will permit. Besides the teaching force already arranged for, it is expected that other medical men, belonging to neighboring stations, will consent to give courses of instruction to the students.

Anyone feeling interested in the above institution may obtain copies of the prospectus in English and Chinese from the writer of this article.

如何激发医学生的科学兴趣

聂会东 著

只要教过中国医学生的老师都发现，这些学生无论是在课堂上还是在实验室，都可以轻松完成日常工作。他们认真按时上课，兢兢业业完成本职工作，但是培养他们对科学的兴趣却很难。据我所知，他们很少要求减免常规课程和实验室工作；但与此同时，他们对刻苦研究缺乏热情，很难提出有见地的问题。

举一个例子。笔者一直对化学充满兴趣，经常在实验室开展无机物分析的课程，并试图让学生通过分析中国商店中的药物以激发他们的兴趣。然而，他们仅仅满足于完成指定的工作，虽然实验室和所有的资源唾手可得，但他们对深入的研究并不感兴趣，他们似乎只愿意从事日常的工作。

同样的问题也出现在与药房和医院有关的工作当中。当要求为病人做检查时，每个学生都会积极参加，集中精力听取病例分析，但老师一转身，他的兴趣就消失了，显得漠不关心，只有极少数的学生会继续关注深入检查病例。如果让他们重新去检查一个病例，如同笔者反复对眼科和皮肤病患者做的那样，虽然大部分情况下他们会做出正确的诊断，但有时他们会因不愿意花时间做详细检查而递交一份非常草率的报告，这表明他们缺乏足够的兴趣来给予病例应有的关注。

现在我们可以做些什么来弥补这些明显的缺点，去激发学生认真探索和细致入微的精神，而不是仅仅停留在日常工作中呢？换句话说，我们需要让他们认识到医学研究不是仅仅从书本中学习，而是需要去关注那些他们管理的病人。

对以上问题，我提出以下建议：

第一，对每个学生进行实验研究方法的全面培训。

在医学课程开始的时候，让学生学好化学、物理学等基础知识，让实验室工作成为每天学习的主要部分。前三年对骨骼进行彻底的研究，并要求学生在骨架上标出书中标注的各个部位，这需要对巴黎人体模型进行仔细研究；让学生学习组织学，在实验室详细讲解，每个学生都需要自己准备切片；在实验室进行生物化学培训；最后要求他们解剖动物，以便熟悉各种组织的形态和身体的结构。

在课程的第二年，让学生在药房实践以认识各种药物的标本，由生理实验室的老师指导。同时练习包扎。

在课程的第三年，希望学生能够在病理组织学方面做一些实验室工作。在病理临床实验室全面培训如何化验血液、尿液等物质，并进行细菌学研究。在课程的第四年和第五年，仍然不能忽视之前提到的实验室工作，但毫无疑问，学生将着重于医院实习，包括临床学术讨论、门诊和医院病房的工作。

第二，让每个学生去管理住院患者。

我的意思是不仅要求学生为患者进行诊断和治疗，而且要依靠自己的判断，完全承担治疗医院住院患者的责任。他们也应该主刀进行手术，并对术后病人进行照顾。我们很容易认为自己比学生和助手了解的多，以至于觉得不能让他们负责重要的病例；而且，我们自己去做比花时间和必要的精力监督学生们工作要快得多。我个人越来越觉察到我自己的弱点：我自己做了实际上应该由助手或者学生完成的事情，而这些事情可以促进他们自己的进步以及中国本土医疗专业人才的发展。

结果证实了我这种观点。我已经不止一次惊讶和高兴地看到学生离开学校投入自己事业以后所做的杰出工作。在课堂上我一直不敢相信他们能有今天的成就，但其实只要给予他们足够的机会，他们能够展示自己的才能。中国人并不缺乏成为好的手术者和临床医生所必须的自信，我们所要做的是在我们的指导下给予他们更多的实践机会，而不是期望他们在离开我们以后再去学习。

第三，有一个医学阅览室。

目前计划中为学生和助理建立医学阅览室所面临的巨大困难是缺乏中文医学期刊,但我们都相信我们尊敬的编辑秘书很快会补充这些缺陷。事实上,在讲课中几乎所有使用新术语的医学书籍都被用来做教科书,在阅览室中,这些书籍并不会给学生带来新的东西。但是一部分在售的旧的医学书籍或许可以作为图书馆的核心。尽管我们的出版委员会发布的整套标准丛书已经在常规课程中作为教材使用,我还是希望能够把它们放在图书馆里以供参考。

第四,我们自己要成为充满热情的科学家。

想要培养学生对于科学的热情和兴趣,我们必须从自身做起,向他们证明科学的价值。据说,伟大的病理学家、宾夕法尼亚大学医学部的弗勒斯纳博士(Dr. Flexner)通过向大家展示自己对科学工作的巨大兴趣,感染了所有与他接触的人,给医学部注入了科研的新活力。

我们有充分的理由满怀激情,因为我们面前有一个不可限量的领域,不仅是以科学方式,更是出于人道主义关怀。我们所处的位置能够在中国做大量的工作发展西医。当每年成千上万的人来到我们面前期望解除病痛,而我们有机会培养他们自己人——在我们这里学习的年轻人为他们自己和人民服务的时候,我相信唤起我们和我们的学生们对于崇高信仰的热情并不困难。我们不仅仅是出于我们的信仰,更是为了在这片遥远的土地上我们所服务的人们,我们为自己和学生设定了这样的标准和目标,这将给我们所代表的事业带来信心,并向人们展示我们不仅能做伟大的人道主义工作,也能做好一流的科学工作。

(摘自 *China Medical Missionary Journal*, 1910, 11:6)

How Can We Stimulate Scientific Interest in Medical Students?

James Boyd Neal, M . D.

No one who has taught Chinese medical students for any length of time can fail to have been impressed with the difficulty of exciting in them the interest he himself naturally feels in scientific subjects. It is easy enough to get them to do their daily work, whether in class room or laboratory. Indeed it is remarkable how regular they invariably are in their attendance and how faithful in the performance of their daily duties; it being a rare thing in the writer's experience to have students ask to be excused from their regular recitations or their laboratory work. At the same time it is by no means easy to beget in them any enthusiasm for the studies which they pursue so assiduously, or to persuade them to ask intelligent questions.

As an instance in point, the writer has always been much interested in chemistry and has regularly had laboratory work for the classes under his care in inorganic analysis, seeking to stimulate interest by having the students do original work in the analysis of inorganic drugs to be found in the Chinese shops. In no instance, however, has he been able to excite sufficient interest in students to do more than the required amount of work, though the laboratory and all its resources have been at their disposal, and though they have seemed to be fairly interested and very faithful in the doing of the daily tasks.

Again the same difficulty appears in connection with dispensary and hospital work. When called to examine a case every student comes with the greatest alacrity and listens to the explanation of the case with gratifying attention, but the instant the instructor's back is turned his interest is gone and he does not seem to care, with rare exceptions, to go on and examine for himself what is to be seen. If again a case is sent to them for diagnosis, as the writer has repeatedly done with eye and skin patients, though frequently a correct diagnosis is reported, sometimes a manifestly snap report is sent back and oftentimes sufficient time has not been taken for making a careful examination, showing that they have not been enough interested to give the case the care it has deserved.

Now what can be done to remedy these manifest defects and to stimulate in our students a spirit of careful inquiry and painstaking attention, not only to their daily duties, but to the patients who come under their care; in other words to eradicate from their minds the idea that the study of medicine is merely a matter of learning from books?

In answer I would make the following suggestions:

First. — Give every student thorough training in laboratory methods.

From the very beginning of his course, that is, his medical course, taking for granted a knowledge of chemistry, physics, etc., let the work in laboratory occupy a very prominent place in the daily drill, giving him in his first 3 year thorough work on the bones, requiring him to demonstrate on the skeleton the various points brought out in the text he is studying, requiring a careful study of good Parisian models of the human body, taking him on through histology, taught exclusively in the laboratory, each student being required to prepare his own sections, and giving him laboratory drill in physiological chemistry, and finally requiring him to do at least some work in the dissection of animals, so as to become familiar with the appearance of the various tissues and the general arrangement of things in the body.

In his second year let him have practical work in pharmacy and in the recognition of specimens in material medical, together with at least demonstrations by an instructor in the physiological laboratory, and practical work in bandaging.

In his third year he will naturally be expected to do some laboratory work in pathological histology, and should be required to take a thorough training in the pathological clinical laboratory in the examination of the urine, blood, etc. and in the study of bacteriology. During the fourth and fifth years, while not neglecting to still keep up his work in the last mentioned laboratory, his practical work will, no doubt, be directed more especially toward clinical conferences, clinics, and service in the wards of the hospital. This leads naturally to the second suggestion, namely:

Second. —Give each student the care of cases in hospital.

By this I mean not merely requiring him to examine and report on the diagnosis and treatment of patients, but also to assume the whole responsibility of certain occupants of the hospital and thus learn to rely on his own judgment. He should also be expected to perform operations on his own responsibility and have the care of them afterwards. How easy it is for us all to feel that we know so much more than our students and assistants that we cannot afford to allow them to treat important cases? And, too, how much quicker it is to thus do the work ourselves than to take the time and the pains necessary to see them do it under our supervision? Personally I feel more and more my own weakness in thus allowing myself to do what students and assistants should be allowed to do for their own good and for the best interests of the native medical profession in China.

Such confidence is justified by the results. I have more than once been surprised and gratified to see what excellent work young men have done after leaving school and when thrown on their own resources, men whom I have been afraid to trust during their course, but who have shown the stuff in them when given a fair chance. The Chinese are not lacking in the self-confidence necessary to make good operators and good clinicians, and it would seem to be our business to give them the chance to acquire more practical experience while under our eye rather than expect them to acquire it all after leaving our care.

Third.—Have a medical reading room.

The great difficult which confronts us in planning for a medical reading room for our students and assistants is the lack of medical journals in Chinese, a lack which we all trust our worthy editorial secretary, will soon be in a position to supply, and the fact that nearly or quite all the medical books issued in the new nomenclature are used as textbooks during the course, so that they do not bring anything new to the student. There are, however, a number of old medical books which I believe are still for sale, which might perhaps serve as a nucleus for such a library.

Then too we should wish to have the whole set of standard works issued by our Publication Committee placed in the library for reference, even though they do most of them appear in the regular course.

Fourth.—Be enthusiastic scientific men ourselves.

It is idle to expect to develop enthusiasm or scientific interest in our students unless we ourselves show them that it is worthwhile. It has been said that Dr. Flexner, the great pathologist, introduced a new spirit into the medical department of the University of Pennsylvania by simply exhibiting himself such an interest in scientific work that he infected all who came into contact with him.

We have every reason for enthusiasm, for we have a practically unlimited field before us, not only in a scientific line but also in a humanitarian way, and are in a position to do immense things in the way of developing scientific medicine in this empire. With thousands and tens of thousands coming to us every year for relief and with the opportunity of training for the service of their own people and their Master these young men and women who are in our care, there should be little difficulty in arousing in ourselves and in our students also an absorbing enthusiasm for and interest in our noble profession. We owe it not only to our profession but to the Master whom we serve in this faraway land to set such standards before ourselves and our students as shall bring credit to the cause we represent, and show people that we not only do good humanitarian work but also first class scientific work.

中国的医学院

聂会东 著

《记录者》杂志曾经约我在其10月份的期刊上发表一篇与医学院校有关的文章，我欣然答应了，因为这是目前摆在中国博医会面前最重要的课题了。此前，博医会在北京召开的最新大会上，大家花费了很多精力讨论如何培养训练有素的合格的基督教医生，最后达成了一致的意见，意见如下：

“博医会目前的最重要的任务是培养基督教男女医生，使他们成为完全合格的医学传教士，并在当地占有一席之地，影响他们所在地的居民，将我们的工作持续进行下去。”

“因此，博医会认为，当前我们应大力推进这一目标，将我们的精力集中在建设博医会批准的联合医学院和设备齐全的医院上。我们强烈建议和其他差会机构联合办学。”

“当前在中国的运动，掀起了国民教育改革的热潮；我们必须认识到，在我们的工作中尽量减少国外元素，学校应逐步增加中国员工，并得到中国人的支持。”

“博医会强烈建议直到下述的联合医科大学配备足够的职工和设备，再开始在中国建立新的医学院。”

“从北方数起，医学院校涉及的城市包括：奉天（Mukden）、北京（Peking）、济南（Tsinan）、成都（Chengtu）、汉口（Hankow）、南京（Nanking）、杭州（Hangchow）、福州（Foochow）和广州（Canton）。（共8个，南京—杭州并为一个）”

“博医会建议应该提供充足的教室和实验室，尽可能地配备显微镜、模型、病理标本等。在最后两年的临床实习中，每个学生应至少负责3个床位的患者。”

“博医会认为，除非有训练有素的护士，否则我们医院的护理工作永远不能令人满意；如果有可能，每一家大型医院都应该有一位训练有素的外国护士，在与医学院开展合作的过程中，护理工作不可或缺。”

根据上述决议，医学院正在上述8所医学教育中心践行决议的精神，即便目前这些学院的员工和设备远低于博医会设定的标准。但是为增加员工和设备所做出的努力却不曾停止，希望能够及时达到规定的标准。迄今为止，只有北京大学接近这一标准，但是他们在提高教职工数量和效率方面也存在困难。

在上述学院中，无法准确地说出有多少在校学生，但估计包括预科生在内，学生人数超过300人。另外，有相当数量的学生仍然在小型医院的课堂中按照旧的教学模式学习，这类学生可能超过200人。所以保守地说，现在大约有500名医学生正在基督教的影响之下，学习西医知识。

本文得以完成，得益于博医会尽可能让医学院的运作符合教育部的规定，同时，在医学教育方面配合并协助政府的工作。

我们所希望的是一个自由、公平的环境，如果我们的学校可以与公立学校一起公平竞争，我们有信心我们的学生能通过考试。

最后，还要提及高似兰医生(Dr. Philip B. Cousland)编辑的系列医学教材，博医会出版委员会正在发行，书籍采用了一些新确定的医学术语，正在修订和再版，希望政府可以留意到此书，并且可能将其作为国家标准术语使用。这一系列书籍几乎涵盖了医学的各主要分支，且还在持续增补中。

Medical Schools in China

James Boyd Neal, M. D.

I have been asked by the "RECORDER" to let it have something on the above subject for its October issue, and I gladly comply with the request, for the reason that no more important subject is now before the China Medical Missionary Association. At its late meeting in Peking a large part of the time of the Association was taken up with the discussion of how best to meet the pressing need for trained Christian doctors, and as a result of the discussions the following resolutions, among others, were passed unanimously:

"A most important feature of the work of Medical Missions in China at the present juncture is the training of Christian young men and women that they may take their place as thoroughly qualified medical missionaries to perpetuate the work we have positions of influence in the service of their country."

"The Association therefore considers that the object of out presence here can now be best advanced by concentrating our energies largely on the important centers approved by the Association and forming there efficient Union Medical Colleges and specially equipped hospitals. And we would strongly recommend that all such colleges be affiliated and co-ordinated with other existing missionary institutions."

"Recent movements in China have developed a national desire among the people to carry out their own educational reforms, and this we must recognize, and make the foreign element in our work as little prominent as possible, by having our colleges gradually and increasingly staffed and supported by the Chinese themselves.

"The association strongly recommends that until the under mentioned Union Medical Colleges are efficiently staffed and equipped no new medical colleges be started in China."

The schools referred to, beginning with the north, are Mukden, Peking, Tsinan, Chengtu, Hankow, Nanking, Hangchow, Foochow, and Canton. (Eight in all, Nanking-Hangchow being one.)

"The Association recommends that ample lecture room and laboratory accommodation should be provided, and as liberal equipment as possible in microscopes, models, pathological specimens, etc., also that clinical opportunities to the extent of three beds to each student in the two final years be considered the minimum.

"The Association is of the opinion that the nursing in our hospitals can never be satisfactory until we have thoroughly trained nurses; that a foreign trained nurse should be associated with each large hospital, whenever possible, and that this should be considered indispensable in those hospitals which are associated with the work of Medical Colleges."

It is in accordance with, and in the spirit of, the above resolutions that schools are now being conducted in all the above eight centers, though the staffing and equipment of these schools is at present far below the standard set by the Medical Missionary Association. Efforts however are being constantly made to increase the staffing and equipment, so that it is hoped in time to reach the standard set in the above actions. So far only the Peking College approximates to this standard, and even there they have constant difficulty in keeping their teaching staff up to the point desired in numbers and efficiency.

It is impossible to say definitely how many are now under instruction in the above schools, but probably, including the preparatory year, something over three hundred. In addition there are a goodly number still being trained according to the old methods in small hospital classes, and these possibly may aggregate two hundred more, so that it seems safe to say that probably five hundred medical students are now getting some knowledge of western medicine under Christian influences.

This paper would not be complete without some reference to the fact that the Medicaid Missionary Association is desirous of bringing its medical schools into line with the regulations of the Ministry of Education, and in all ways to co-operate with and assist the Government in Medical Education.

All we desire is a free field and no favor, feeling confident that if we are allowed to compete on equal terms with government schools our students will be able to stand the test of the government examinations.

In closing, mention should be made of the series of medical text-books, which under the editorship of Dr. Phillip B. Cousland, is being issued by the Publication Committee of the Association, and which embraces the new medical terms adopted some time since, and now being revised and re-issued in the hope that the Government may take favorable notice of them, and possibly adopt them as the standard nomenclature of the country. The series now includes books covering nearly all the main branches of medicine and is being constantly added to.

中国的联合医科大学

聂会东 著

自1900年义和团运动以后，外国差会联合教育工作又恢复正轨，与此同时，大规模的运动正以联合办学为方向，如火如荼地进行着。例如，长老会、公理会及伦敦差会在北京(Peking)的联合办学；四川(Szechuan)教会间的联合办学，山东(Shantung)的美国长老会和英国浸礼会之间的联合办学。

人们在联合办学方面有着强烈的愿望，希望通过联合办学为中国培养出一群基督徒医生，在中国不同地区已建成的联合医学院中，联合教育已初见成效。

最广为人知的，也是迄今为止这些医学院中最大的——北京的协和医科学院，除了上面提到的三个传教会，中华圣公会和卫理公会也参与了办学。从明年开始，他们将招收超过100名学生。学校得到了政府的认可，承诺学生毕业时将得到中国政府颁发的毕业证书，这对于他们在陆军或海军中获得职位大有裨益。

在中国的中心城市汉口(Hankow)，有一所新的联合医科学院开始建设，如果能得到董事会和社会团体的全力支持，未来无疑将在医学教育方面做出巨大的贡献。目前，主要由伦敦差会推动建设这个项目。

南京(Nanking)的联合医学院也正在建立中，但至今尚未真正开始培养医生。

在遥远的南方城市广州(Canton)，宾夕法尼亚大学正在为建设一所医科大学做准备，希望这个医学院在将来能够为南方的医学教育做出贡献。同时，男子医学院与教会慈善医院和长老会夏葛(E. A. K Hackett)女子医学院联合在一起。它们都是联合办学的性质。

依我看来，耶鲁大学肩负教育使命，在中国中部的湖南省(the Province of Hunan)——正筹划建立一所高水准的医科大学；而哈佛大学也正准备在福州建立一所设备齐全的医科大学。

最后，我们山东长老会与英国浸礼会就联合教育进行了协商，将于 1910 年 3 月 1 日在济南开办联合医学院。几年来，在没有获得联合学院办学地点及宿舍的建造的这段时间中，两个教会的传教医生一直在开展联合医学教育。办学地点定于济南南部郊区，坐落在城市发展最迅速的区域，学校目前还在建设中，有很大希望能在明年年初入驻。三层的主楼将有足够的教室和实验室。同时还将建立一所现代化设施的能够提供临床和手术指导的医院和学生宿舍。

学校由在伦敦的浸礼会艾宗敦（Arthington）基金资助建设，建筑物属于英国浸礼会，但是学校的运转由美国长老会和英国浸礼会成立的联合委员会管理。

我们满怀信心地期待山东其他差会加入我们的联合教育。

正如联盟所描述的，学校建立的目标和原则是“在基督教的影响下，主要对来自基督教家庭的青年人给予医学教育”。同时，也欢迎来自非基督教家庭的品德优良、符合要求的青年人入学。

学生需要支付住宿伙食费、书费、旅行等相关费用，此外每年还需支付 10 墨西哥银元的学费。

山东省有 20 000 多名基督教徒，在省会济南，我们计划开设的教育机构将有广阔的发展前景。我们一开学就有大约 25 名青年准备入学。

[摘自 *The Christen Work*, 1915, 98(1)]

Union Medical Colleges in China

James Boyd Neal, M. D.

Ever since the Boxer year, 1900, the subject of union in educational work has been much to the foreign missionary circles in China, and large movements are now in progress in that direction, such, for instance, as the union in educational work in Peking between the Presbyterians, Congregationalists and the London Mission; the union in the great Province of Szechuan between several missions in education, and the union in Shantung between the American Presbyterians and the English Baptists.

Either connected with such general movements, or independent of them, there has been shown a great desire to unite in the training of a body of Christian doctors for China, and the fruits are already beginning to show in a number of Union Medical Colleges in different parts of the empire.

The most well known, and so far the largest of these, is the Union Medical College in Peking, which, in addition to the three missions mentioned above, has also the Anglican Mission and the Methodist Mission interested in it. With the beginning of next year they will have over one hundred students enrolled. They have secured government recognition with a promise that their graduates shall receive diplomas from the Chinese government, which will be a great help to them in securing positions in the army or navy.

At Hankow, in the very center of the country, there is a new Union Medical College started, which in the future will undoubtedly do an immense work in the line of medical education, provided it is liberally supported by the boards and societies interested in it. At present the London Mission is the principal one interested in pushing it forward.

At Nanking a promising union movement is in progress, but so far has not yet actually begun the work of training doctors.

At Canton, in the far south, the University of Pennsylvania is laying the foundations of a medical college which all hope will in the future do a large work for medical education in that part of the country. While in the same city, in connection with the Broad Benevolent Hospital, there is a medical school for men, and in connection with the Presbyterian Board's work the E. A. K. Hackett Medical College for women. Both of these are in the nature of union schools.

In Central China, Yale, in connection with its educational mission, which is intended to do the higher work in that line for all missions working in the Province of Hunan, is planning to start a medical college, while Harvard, too, is preparing to inaugurate a well equipped medical college somewhere in Central China—at Foochow, I believe.

Lastly, we Presbyterians here in Shantung, in connection with our educational union with the English Baptists, opened in Tsinan a Union Medical College, the first of March, 1910. For several years union medical classes have been carried on by the medical men of the two missions concerned, pending the obtaining of a site and the erection of buildings for the accommodation of the union college. Such a site was secured last year in the south suburb of Tsinan, in the most rapidly growing section of the city, and buildings are now in course of construction which, it is confidently hoped, will be ready for occupancy early next year. The main three-story building will provide ample accommodation for lecture rooms and laboratories for practical study. A modern equipped hospital will give facilities for instruction in clinical medicine and surgery, and dormitories will also be built.

The whole plant is being provided by the Baptist Missionary Society in London from grants made by the trustees of the Arthington Fund, but while the buildings belong to the English Baptist Mission, the college is a union institution under the joint control of the two missions concerned, through a union board of directors.

It is confidently anticipated that other Protestant missions in Shantung will share in this union.

The aim and policy of the college, as stated in the Basis of Union, will be: "To give medical education, under distinctively Christian influences, to young men chiefly from Christian families." At the same time young men from non-Christian families will be admitted provided they are able to meet the requirements, are of good character, and are willing to abide by the rules of the institution.

Students will be required to meet all expenses connected with their board, books, travel, etc., and in addition pay a tuition fee of ten Mexicans a year.

With a Christian constituency of over 20,000 church members in the Province of Shantung, it is felt that there is a wide field for just such an institution as we are planning to open soon in Tsinan, the capital of the province. About twenty-five young men are ready to enter as soon as we open our doors.

记章嘉礼的一次来访

聂会东 著

我很高兴给你讲述一些章嘉礼夫妇(Dr. and Mrs. Johnson)来济南府(Chinanfu)访问的事情。但是遗憾的是,他们只能在这里待 2 天,更遗憾的是,第二天章嘉礼博士(Dr. Johnson)因喉炎发作说不出话来,只能取消了第二天的部分安排,与此有关的人都因此感到有些失落。尽管有这些遗憾,他们在这里的访问是非常有益且鼓舞人心的,并让我们都相信此次访问意义深远。他们在的这两天,中国人的例会在每天早上举行,在第二天的例会上,所有尚未成为基督徒的人都被邀请站起来并当众宣布他们将成为耶稣基督的追随者。20 多人回应了这一邀请,其中包括 10 至 12 名来自男子学院的学生和 10 名在场的医学班的学生。晚上,由莫约翰(Murray)先生主持的会议上(章嘉礼博士无法参加),又进行了早晨的邀请,我敢说所有早会站出来的人,还有包括医学班剩下的 2 个人在内的其他人,他们之前从未表明加入基督教,但这次都宣誓加入基督教。我应该提一下,在 8 点半的早会结束以后,医学班和男子学校的学生为了有更多的时间来祷告而请了当天的假。所以当天极虔诚的祷告充分抒发了圣灵精神,祷告不仅仅在数十个学生的心灵转换中起效,而且对于那些已经成为基督徒的人的精神是一种强化,同时鼓舞所有教会人员拥有更加虔诚的灵魂。

最近人们对于当地教堂的兴趣明显增加,大约 25 个人在章嘉礼博士到来之前请求获准进入教堂,他的到来以及他鼓舞人心的演讲有助于加深和拓宽基督教的传播,尤其是激发我们学生的兴趣,他们似乎成为最大的受益者。这次访问已经极大地鼓舞了我们,我们仍然希望此次访问将会带来更好的结果。

[摘自 *The Chinese Recorder and Missionary Journal*, 1906, 37(1)]

Chinanfu

James Boyd Neal, M. D.

I am glad to send you some account of the visit of Dr. and Mrs. Johnson in Chinanfu. Unfortunately they could spare only two days to us here, and still more unfortunately on the second day Dr. Johnston was so disabled with an attack of laryngitis that he could not speak above a whisper, so was compelled to give up several engagements on the second day, much to the disappointment of everybody concerned. Notwithstanding these drawbacks, however, their visit here was most helpful and inspiring and has led to results which we all trust will be permanent. General meetings for the Chinese were held in the morning of each day they were here, and at the meeting on the second day an invitation was given to all who were not already Christians to rise and make public declaration of their intention to become followers of Jesus Christ. In response to this invitation some twenty or more rose, including ten or a dozen from the Boys' Academy and one of the class of ten medical students who are now here. In the evening, at a meeting conducted by Mr. Murray in the absence of Dr. Johnston, the invitation of the morning was repeated, and I believe all who had risen in the morning and some others, including the remaining two of the medical class who had never professed Christ, rose and indicated their intention to live the Christian life. I should say that after the meeting of the morning, which was held at half-past eight, the medical class requested that they be excused from the regular work of the day, so that they might spend more time in prayer, and the same was true of the boys' school, so that during that day much earnest prayer was offered for an outpouring of the Holy Spirit, prayer which seems to have been answered not only in the conversion of a goodly number of the students, but in the deepening of the spiritual life of those who were already Christians and in the stirring up of a more earnest spirit among the church-members generally.

There has lately been a rather marked interest in the local church here; some twenty-five having applied some time before the coming of Dr. Johnston for admission to the church, and his coming and his earnest in spring talks have helped to deepen and greatly broaden this spirit, and especially to enlist the interest of our students, for they seem to have been the ones who have received most benefit. We are hoping for still further good results from this visit, which we feel has already been greatly blessed to us here.

山东济南联合医学院和医院

聂会东夫人伊丽莎白 著

美国长老会、英国浸礼会和圣公会在山东开展联合教育工作已经有 10 多年了。山东省和邻近省份的其他差会正在考虑加入这个联盟,并派人到山东基督教大学的三个学院任教。现在他们只是输送学生。

在这三个学院中,有着精良的、宽敞的、新型的建筑和设备的艺术学院,是由我们的长老会提供的。神学院和医学院的建筑归英国浸礼会所有,这三个学院都位于济南。

1909 年,医学院正式成立。1914 年 1 月,在经过 1 年预科学习和 5 年严格的医学和外科学学习后,第一批 4 名合格的年轻基督教医生毕业。顺便说一下,他们来自于 4 个不同的教会,分别是圣公会、公理会、卫理公会和长老会。6 月,又有 3 名因生病或其他原因在第一次考试中未能通过的学生获得了梦寐以求的文凭。次年 1 月,第二批 6 名学生毕业。现在五个班级的学生有 50 多人。

医学院的教员中有我们长老会的聂会东医生、舒尔茨医生(Schultz)、章嘉礼医生;英国浸礼会的巴慕德医生、威廉·弗理明医生(Dr. William Fleming);以及两位从该校毕业的中国人吴医生和杨医生。

尽管在 1909 年第一座教学楼才建成,但自 1886 年以来,聂会东医生和其他在山东的医生在非常困难的条件下,除了进行正常的医疗工作外,一直在不同的传教站给各班级的学生教授课程。现在终于有校舍了,虽然并不完善,但比前几年好多了,我们觉得多年的希望快要实现了。医院 1914 年开始修建;1915 年 9 月 27 日,一位军官主持了开幕典礼。一位在场的人员是这样记录的:

“我们认为医院的开张是一个巨大的成功。建筑和设备都很好,门诊楼也很好。许多官员到场,一切都很完美。在接下来的 5 个早晨,我们分别为商业公司、学校、回民、女士和教会成员举行了接待会。接待会在门诊的等候室举行，由一位军官主持。我们集合在医院的门前，一位军官用银色的钥匙打开了大门。参观完整个建筑，我们集合在一个病房，发表讲话，然后拍了一张合影，接待会结束。”

这家医院有 100 张床位。

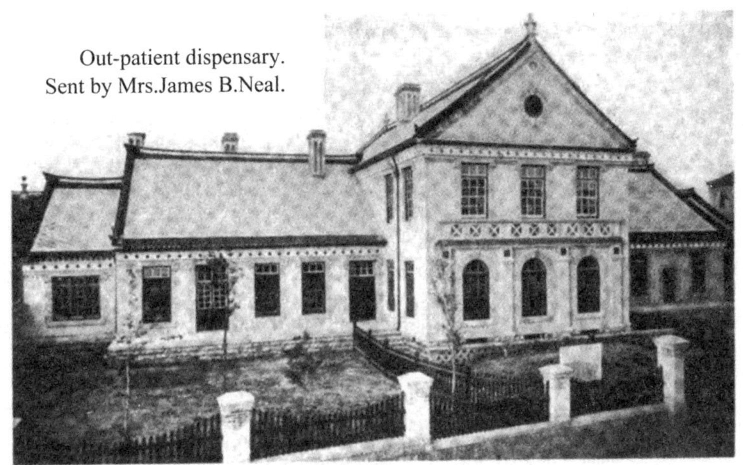

医院门诊楼

（摘自 *Woman's foreign Missionary Societies of the Prebyterian Church*，1916）

Union Medical School and Hospital at Tsinan, Shantung

Elizabeth S. Neal.

In Shantung we have had a union of the American Presbyterian, English Baptist and Anglican Missions in educational work for more than ten years. Other missions, both in Shantung and nearby provinces are considering the proposal to join this Union and to send men to teach in the three departments of the Shantung Christian University. They are now sending students only.

Of the three departments the Arts College with its fine, large, new plant and equipment is being provided by our own Presbyterian Church. The theological and medical departments are the property of the English Baptist Mission, and all three are to be located in Tsinan.

There in 1909 the Medical School building was formally opened. And there in January, 1914, its first class of four fully qualified young Christian physicians was graduated, after one year of study in branches preparatory to medicine and five years of strictly medical and surgical studies. And, by the way, they represented four different missions, Anglican, Congregational, Methodist and Presbyterian. In June three more students, who on account of illness or other reasons failed to pass their first examinations, received the much-coveted diplomas. Next January six more should graduate from the second class. There are over fifty students now in the five classes.

The faculty of the Medical School is composed of Dr. James Boyd Neal, Dr. William M. Schultz and Dr. Charles F. Johnson of our Presbyterian Mission; Dr. Harold Balme and Dr. William Fleming, representing the English Baptist Church, and two Chinese doctors, graduates of the school, Dr. Wu and Yang.

Though it was 1909 before a school building was realized, since the year 1886 Dr. Neal and other Shantung physicians had been teaching classes of students in their different stations in addition to their regular medical work and under very difficult conditions. When at last a school home was provided, with an equipment which, though imperfect, is so much better than that of former years, we felt that the hopes of many years were nearing fulfilment. There, in 1914, the Hospital was begun, and on September twenty seventh, 1915, it was opened by the military Governor. One who was present writes:

"The Hospital opening was, we think, a great success. The building and equipment are really excellent and the out-patient building is fine. Many officials came and the whole thing was fine. On the five mornings following we had receptions for business firms, schools, Mohammedans, ladies and for church members. The reception was held in the waiting room of the dispensary and then, led by the military Governor, we all marched over to the front door of the hospital, which was opened by the military Governor with a silver key. After parading over the entire building we assembled in one of the wards, had addresses, then a photograph taken and it was all over."

The hospital has one hundred beds for patients.

信　件

聂会东博士给博医会的信

聂会东 著

应吉佛瑞医生(Dr. Jefferys)医生的要求,我写了下面这封信向中国博医会阐述几个目前大家都很关心的问题:

一、医学统计

由于这是今年年底前订阅人能收到的最后一期杂志,似乎很适合提醒协会成员注意,协会希望大家能将他们去年的工作统计数据提交给杂志编辑用于发表。然而,令人伤心的是:据我所知,我们目前没有,也从来没有一个完整且可靠的在中国所有的医院和诊所的名单,也没人知道我们医院历年的总接诊量是多少。1900年,我们曾尝试收集在中国所有医疗工作的统计数据,但结果令人失望;尽管发出的表格是经过精心设计将填写表格的麻烦降至最低的,然而还是只有43家医院提交了报告。倘若这次尝试能够成功取得全国各省的回复,本可以形成一个宝贵的基础数据,用于比较义和团运动之后的几年内医疗事业的发展情况,因为义和团运动爆发导致许多医院遭到破坏。

毫无疑问,我们中大多数人都按照公历年来保存记录。似乎需要再多花一点点时间给编辑发一个简短的说明,按照以下项目名称提供我们的年度工作数据,包括"门诊总人次数"(如果方便的话这个部分可以再分成"新病人"与"旧病人")、"住院病人数""出诊数""大手术统计"等等。

对我们自己、我们的同事和支持者,我们有义务让世界知道我们在做什么。我相信,将我们在这个广阔的国家中年复一年完成的工作翔实地记录下来,会给我们医学传教会的每个朋友留下深刻印象并带来帮助。

二、命名法

协会委员会将采用的解剖学、生理学等学科的命名术语列表发布，迄今为止已经2年多了。据作者所知，在杂志的专栏及委员会工作中的私人信件里，很少有批评之声。我们期望对培养医学生或是对编辑医学书籍感兴趣的所有人都能自由地对这些术语提出指正。希望看到这项工作尽快完成的人可以给惠亨通(Whitney)主席或者高似兰(Cousland)秘书写信，告诉他们对此事的意见并敦促完成。委员会是为协会服务的，只有协会成员对委员会正在进行的工作表现出真正的兴趣，他们才会有动力加快进度。命名法的工作应该尽快完成，这样才能对现有的老版本教材进行修订并发行新版教材。我们目前大量的医学教科书中，最有用的一本是嘉约翰博士(Dr. Kerr)的《医学实践》。这是一本非常好的书，但却亟需修订，因为它已经出版超过20年了。谁能想象现在采用的教科书是一本20年前编著且从未修订过的版本？然而如果没有命名委员会提出的与解剖学和生理学中已采用的术语统一的、新的命名，这些书籍也无法得到修订。加快术语命名工作的另一个原因是新版的《格氏解剖学》已经在印刷中，并且一本新的生理学书籍也即将出版，只有临床实践及手术中的术语尽快确定，相关的书籍才可以被修订。不然我们的学生将会处于尴尬的境地：在解剖等基础学科中学习新的术语，在更偏重临床实践的学科中却学习旧的术语，这样会给学生们带来极大的困惑。

三、明年的协会会议是否召开

协会近13年以来一直没有再开过任何会议，我们期望在不久的将来可以召集一次协会会议，但是能不能定在明年尽快会晤还是一个问题。在第12期杂志的197页有一个可能会在协会会议上被讨论的主题的简短列表；当然感兴趣的同事也会想到其他主题。协会的成员们会非常高兴地听取各个会员对这些问题有什么期望。如果鼓岭(Kuling)和其他地方的会议能够不时地取得成功，召开全体会议将会是很有益的，也能取得地方会议所无法达到的成果。5 年一次的总会应该定期召开，从时间上来看也不至于太过频繁。

聂会东

［摘自 *China Medical Missionary Journal*, 1903, 17(1)］

Presidents' Letter

At the request of Dr. Jefferys, I am writing the following letter to lay before the China Medical Missionary Association a few matters which seem of timely interest just at the present moment:—

First. Medical Statistics

As this is the last number of the JOURNAL which will reach subscribers before the end of the current year, it seems fitting to call the attention of the numbers of the Association to the desirability of sending to the editors of the JOURNAL statistics of their work during the past year for publication. It is a melancholy fact that there is not now, and never has been, so far as my knowledge goes, a reliable and full list of all hospitals and dispensaries in China, nor does anyone know what the aggregate attendance at our hospitals has been in any year. An attempt was made in 1900 to collect the statistics of all medical work in the empire, but the results were most disappointing; only forty-three hospitals reporting, though special blanks were sent out, so arranged as to require the minimum of trouble in filling in. If this attempt to collect the returns from all the provinces had been successful it would have formed a valuable basis for comparison with the development during the years succeeding the great Boxer outbreak, when so many hospitals were destroyed.

Most of us, no doubt, keep our records according to the calendar year, and it would seem to require a very small expenditure of time to send a brief note to the editors giving them the figures of our year's work, under such heads as "Total Number of Attendances of Out patients," dividing this head, if convenient, into "New" and "Old," "Number of Hospital In-patients," "Out-calls," "Major Operations," etc.

Do we not owe it to ourselves, our colleagues, and our supporters to let the world know what we are doing? I am confident that a truthful statement of what is being accomplished from year to year, in the line of medical missionary work in this vast empire, would be most impressive and helpful of every friend to medical missions.

Second. Nomenclature

It is now over two years since the list of terms adopted by the Association's Committee on Nomenclature in anatomy, physiology, etc. , was sent out, and so far there has been, so far as known to the writer, very little criticism either in the columns of the Journal or in private letters of the work of the committee. It is very desirable that these terms should be criticised very freely by all those who are interested in the training of medical students or the making of medical books. It will also be well if those who are anxious to see the work go on to completion will write to the chairman of the committee, Dr. Whitney, or to Dr. Cousland, the secretary, urging upon them their wishes in the matter. The committee is the servant of the Association, and unless the members of the Association show a real interest in the work the committee is trying to do, there is little encouragement to hurry up matters. It seems eminently desirable that this work in nomenclature should be pushed to a conclusion as speedily as possible, so as to allow of the revision of old editions of existing textbooks and to facilitate the issue of new ones. One of the most useful of our present lot of medical textbooks is Dr. Kerr's *Practice of Medicine*, a most excellent book, but one which is greatly in need of revision, as it is now over twenty years old. Who would think nowadays of studying a book written twenty years ago, and not revised since, and yet how can the book under discussion be revised until the Nomenclature Committee gives the revisers new terms consistent with those already adopted in anatomy and physiology?

Another reason for hurrying up the work on nomenclature is that already a new edition of *Gray's Anatomy* is in press and a new physiology will soon be ready for publication, and unless the terms in practice and surgery are soon ready, so these books can be revised, our students will be placed in the embarrassing position of learning the new terms in these preliminary branches and the old ones in the more practical branches, thereby leading to great confusion.

Third. Shall we have a meeting of the Association next year?

As it is already thirteen years since there has been any meeting of the Association it would seem desirable that we should meet some time in the near future, but whether or not we can meet so soon as next year is a question. On page 197 of Vol. XVI of the Journal will be found a short list of subjects which might profitably come up for discussion at a meeting of the Association; those interested will doubtless think of others. The officers of the Association will be very glad to hear from individual members what their wishes in the matter are. If the conferences at Kuling and elsewhere can be made such a success from time to time, surely a general meeting should be quite as profitable, and would have the authority to accomplish tangible results which the local meetings lack. A meeting of the general association once in five years could surely be arranged and would certainly not be too frequent.

J. B. Neal

聂会东主席的信

聂会东 著

全中国的协会成员请特别注意刊登在本期的明年冬天在上海举办协会会议的正式通知。这个会议是在与执行委员会成员协商后决定的，该委员会由协会的负责人和其他相关成员组成。正如读者通讯栏所述，协会的苏州（Soochow）分会要求在传教士全体大会期间安排一次会议，此后每 2～3 年举行一次。由于近 3 年内不会再举行大会，而且我们的医疗传教工作中有许多亟待解决的问题，我们认为最好能在明年再召开一次会议，并且期望在 1907 年再举行一次会议，之后，我们可能会决定每 2～3 年举行一次大会。文恒理博士（Boone）、赖芙斯纳德博士（Dr. Reifsnyder）和吉佛瑞博士（Jefferys）已同意担任上海地方组织委员会委员，针对讨论主题等的建议都应该尽早发送给他们，或者更确切地说是发送给担任委员会秘书的吉佛瑞博士。委员会欢迎任何对即将到来的会议有帮助及有益的建议。诚挚地希望协会的每一位成员都能够用心准备这次会议，不仅仅是出席会议，更要尽一切可能使之成功。从上次 1890 年的会议到现在我们再次相聚已将近 15 年时间，因此我们应该有许多可讨论的话题。

协会成员

我建议大家在接下来的几个月里共同努力，吸纳在中国的每一位医学传教士成为协会会员。这样在会议召开时我们就会形成一个统一的阵线，也可以向外界表明虽然成员分散在中国各处，但医学传教士团体是一支不可小觑的力量。我们大家都知道每个新成员的加入都意味着协会收入的增加，每年收取 3 美元的会费，其中包括订阅期刊费用，这样我们就可以开展一些因缺少资金而无法开展的工作。例如，中文医学术语词典就需在确定术语命名后尽快出版。

命名委员会

命名委员会过去5周一直在上海工作，很好地完成了余下的术语列表，这些术语涵盖了内科、外科、眼科和皮肤科、妇产科，还有外科器械和手术，并制订了命名药物学方面术语的计划。所有以上列表，有望在几个月内发布，真诚地希望那些对统一制定术语感兴趣的人，特别关注一下这些术语，并在明年的大会上提出指正。到目前为止，只有一人对之前在1901年出版的《解剖学》《生理学》等著作中的术语提出过指正，因此，很难知道这一工作是否会得到协会的认同。在即将举行的会议上，最重要的一件事就是接收命名委员会的报告并确定术语。大家应该清楚地认识到，在1901和今年制定的术语表就是为了接受修正而发布的，而且在我们协会通过并决定采用之前，它们也决不是最终的或权威的版本。

即将出版的医学书籍

那些对医学生培养感兴趣的人会很高兴听到以下消息，惠亨通博士(Dr. Whitney)一直致力于《格氏解剖学》新译本的出版；同时，高似兰博士(Dr. Cousland)也正在出版一本新的、非常急需的《生理学》，也就是《哈氏生理学》的译本，之前使用的是柯克(Kirke)的书。这两位译者都使用了委员会在1901发表的新术语，这样那些想在实际使用中考察新术语的协会会员，书籍一出版就请尽快订阅，并在医学生的教学中试用吧。

住在北京附近通州(Tungchow)的盈亨利(Dr. Ingram)，也正在准备一本新的《治疗学》，翻译自贺德(Hare)的著作，在这其中也能看到新的术语；最后纪立生博士(Dr. Gillison)即将发行一部新版《化学》的第一册，其中收录使用了由教育协会委员会和博医会共同商榷的化学术语。我们现在迫切需要做的，是对嘉约翰医生的《医学实践》进行新的修订(或者是重新进行翻译)，用这本书和一本新的《外科学》来取代那些已经过时的书。据说梅藤更博士(Dr. Main)在准备翻译《卡-凯氏外科便览》，这本书对实践工作非常有用，但除此之外，我们应该有一本更详细的书来用于系统教学。

恳请那些已经在从事医学书籍翻译或者正在考虑这样做的同事，与命名委员会秘书，汕头(Swatow)潮州府(Chaochow Fu)的高似兰博士联系一下，防止做重复的工作。

聂会东　上海

1904年3月5日

[摘自 *China Medical Missionary Journal*, 1903, 17(1)]

President's Letter

The attention of members of the Association throughout China is particularly called to the Official Notice in this issue of the coming meeting of the Association in Shanghai next winter. This action was decided upon after consultation with the members of the Executive Committee, which is composed of the officers of the Association and with other members who were within reach. As will be seen by reference to the Correspondence columns, the local branch of the Association in Soochow has asked that a meeting be arranged for during the time of the General Conference of Missionaries, and thereafter at intervals of two or three years. As the next General Conference will not be held for three years, and as there are a number of questions pressing for decision in connection with our medical missionary work, it was thought best to call a meeting within the next year, with the expectation that at the time of the General Conference in 1907 another meeting may be held, after which possibly we may decide to hold either biennial or triennial meetings. Drs. Boone, Reifsnyder, and Jefferys have kindly consented to act as a local Committee of Arrangements in Shanghai, and to them, or rather to Dr. Jefferys, who will act as Secretary of the Committee, all suggestions as to subjects for discussion, etc. , should be sent at as early a date as possible. The Committee will welcome any suggestions whatever which will be likely to add to the interest and increase the benefit to be derived from the coming meeting. It is earnestly hoped that every member of the Association will bear this meeting on his or her heart and will not only plan to be present at it, but will do everything possible to make it a success. It will have been nearly fifteen years since the last meeting in 1890, by the time we get together again, so there should be no lack of subjects for discussion.

Membership of the Association

In this connection may I suggest that a united effort be made to enroll every medical missionary in China as a member of our Association within the next few months, so that we may present a united front when we next meet, and may be able to show clearly what a force the medical missionary body is in China, scattered though it is over this vast empire. It might be well to remember too that every fresh recruit means so much added to the income of the Association, through the annual dues of three dollars, which includes the subscription to the Journal, thus making it possible to undertake work which would otherwise be impossible for lack of funds, such for example as the publishing of a dictionary of medical terms in Chinese, which will be needed as soon as the terms are definitely settled.

Nomenclature Committee

This Committee has been at work in Shanghai during the past five weeks, and has pretty well completed the remaining lists, consisting of terms for Medical and Surgical Diseases, Eye and Skin Diseases, Gynecological and Obstetrical terms, and lists of Surgical Instruments and Operations, and has made plans for the Materia Medica terms. All the above lists, it is hoped, will be ready for distribution within a few months, and it is earnestly hoped that those who are specially interested in the formation of a uniform vocabulary will give particular attention to these terms and be prepared to criticise them at the meeting of the Association next winter. So far, with the exception of one man, there has been little criticism of their former list of terms in Anatomy, Physiology, etc., published in 1901, sent into the Committee, so that it is very difficult to know whether or not their work meets the approval of the Association. At the coming meeting one of the most serious matters of business will be the reception of the report of this Nomenclature Committee and the determination of what shall be done with it. It should be clearly understood that the lists published in 1901 and again this year are issued for criticism, and are by no means final or authoritative until passed upon by the Association and adopted as its own.

Forthcoming Medical Books

Those who are interested in the training of medical students will be glad to know that Dr. Whitney is steadily at work putting his new translation of Gray's Anatomy through the press, and that Dr. Cousland is also publishing a new and much-needed *Physiology*, a translation of *Halliburton's Handbook of Physiology* (formerly known as Kirke's). Both these translators are using the new terms published by the committee in 1901, so that members of the Association who may wish to test the new terms in actual use could not do better than order copies of these books as soon as ready and try them in the teaching of their medical students.

Dr. Ingram, of Tungchow, near Peking, is also preparing a new *Therapeutics*, a translation of Hare's well-known book, in which the new terms will also find a place, and finally Dr. Gillison is about to issue the first volume of a new *Chemistry*, which will embody the chemical terms as determined by the Committee of the Educational Association and the Committee of the Medical Missionary Association acting together. What we urgently need just now is a fresh revision of Kerr's *Practice of Medicine*, brought down to date (or else a perfectly new translation of a good practice) and a new *Surgery* to replace the poor books which are now out of date. Dr. Main is said to be preparing a translation of *Caird and Cathcart's Surgical Handbook*, which will be most useful for practical work, but in addition we should have a more elaborate book for systematic teaching.

Would it not be well for any who may be already engaged in the translation of medical books, or who are contemplating doing so, to communicate with Dr. Cousland, Chaochow Fu, Swatow, the Secretary of the Nomenclature Committee, so as to prevent overlapping in such work?

James B. Neal

Shanghai, March 5th, 1904

来自于出版委员会的信

中国博医会报的编辑们：

尊敬的先生们：我很抱歉推迟了这么久才对孟合理博士(Dr. McAll)在杂志11月刊上对出版委员会工作的礼貌评价作出回复。我很高兴出版委员会的工作能被注意到，哪怕是以批评的方式，至少表明有人对这件事感兴趣，并且在关注着委员会的工作。

首先，我想让孟合理博士注意到这样一个事实，就是他信中提到的在会刊19卷第104页上的所谓的决议，是他的同事纪立生博士(Dr. Gillison)准备的一篇论文的一部分，并在1905年2月的医学会议上进行了宣读。但这并不是官方决议，而只是作者认为的一种可行的方法。官方召开了会议，任命了出版委员会，并制定了行动纲领，这份纲领可以在19卷第43和44页上看到。出版委员会最终决议如下：

(1)我们向协会建议出版标准系列中文教科书，并在切实可行的情况下出版一本中文医学杂志。

(2)成立的出版委员会由以下成员组成：(以下是委员的名字)。

(3)协会每年年底可使用的剩余资金，4/5供委员会使用，委员会也有权通过自愿捐款的方式筹集资金；这些基金都会交付给协会财务部。

委员会没有达成除上述外的协议。但是，我们很赞同孟合理博士的建议，如果建议能付诸实施的话确实是一个不错的方法。他的建议是委员会要全面关注美国和英国出版的全部医学教科书，并选出最好的，然后任命一些人来翻译这些精选的书籍。但是，不幸的是委员会的工作是完全凭个人自愿的，并且是在完成本人本职工作后的业余时间完成。任何委员会的成员都无法拿出1/4的时间用在出版工作上，委员会没有权力要求成员去做他们认为应该做的工作，也没有资金支持经常性的会议来讨论最佳决策。

在这种情况下，唯一可行的似乎只能是接受由执行和编辑委员会通过和提供的书籍，并通过修订和再版来改进现有书籍。我们在处理广州博医会书籍版权的问题上做得非常明智，事实上，我们首先想到的是把它们全部买下来，但没有达成。因为大家都知道，广州发行的书在整个帝国都有销售，而有些我们并不想引进作为标准系列丛书。其他的，像《医学实践》，则是很优秀的书籍，在过去的20年或更长的时间里，在培养医学生方面发挥了很大作用。所以如果这些实用的书籍可以重新修订并更新，也就是保留旧的内容，然后引进新的适用于现在的内容，这难道不是一件明智的事情吗？广州方面已经同意我们选择想要的任何一本书，在彼此的监督下修订和出版，他们可以获得50％的净利润。目前只有嘉约翰博士(Dr. Kerr)的《医学实践》被选中进行这种修订。

第二，高似兰博士(Dr. Cousland)对《欧氏内科学》的翻译，最初由他本人提出，继而得到了委员会成员的衷心支持，因为这是一本很优秀的书，是委员会都熟知的。毫无疑问，其他人可能会有个人偏好，就像孟合理博士偏爱泰勒(Taylor)的书那样，如果我们能够聚在一起进行比较，我们或许能选择一本比《欧氏内科学》更好的书，但是，当委员会因为选择了一本标准用书而被指责时是相当令人为难的。

第三，对于普外科书籍，还没有作出任何决定，可以接受大家的意见。然而，无论如何，都没有想过要修订嘉约翰的《外科学》，这是广东系列中质量最差的一本书。委员会列入其中的唯一一本书是梅藤更博士(Dr. Main)翻译的《卡-凯氏外科便览》，甚至这本都没有最终通过，因为梅藤更博士太忙了，以致于无法使其成形以接受委员会的考证。

最后,我想说以下是目前为止委员会最终决定并已经出版或正在印刷的书目:

1. 高似兰翻译的《哈氏生理学》,译自哈利伯顿(Haliburton)。

2. 盈亨利(Ingram)翻译的《贺氏疗学》,译自贺德和伍德(Hare & Wood)。

3. 富玛利(Fulton)翻译的《妇科疾病学》,译自彭罗斯(Penrose)。

4. 赖马西(Niles)翻译的《伊氏产科学》,译自伊大卫(Evans)等。

5. 聂会东的《眼科证治》。

6. 聂会东的《皮肤证治》。

7. 赖马西对嘉约翰《医学实践》的修订版。

维纳布尔(Venable)的《细菌学》和高似兰翻译的《欧氏内科学》翻译已经得到了委员会的通过,但还没有印刷,直至协会下次会议后才会进行印刷。在汉口翻译的《护士手册》已经提交给协会,但是还没有被通过。在4月即将召开的会议上,协会将有机会讨论出版委员会的工作,我们相信会是一个充分的、自由的讨论,委员会可能会因为一些实际的建议而得到很大的帮助,因为委员会正准备出版系列中文医学标准教科书。

敬上

聂会东
出版委员会主席
济南,1907.1.17

[摘自 *China Medical Missionary Journal*, 1907, 1(1)]

From the Publication Committee.

Tsinan, January 17th, 1907

Editors *China Medical Missionary Journal*:

Dear Sirs: I am sorry to have delayed so long in sending you an answer to Dr. McAll's courteous criticism in the November number of the Journal of the work of the Publication Committee. It is a pleasure to have the work of the committee noticed even in the way of criticism, for it shows that some are taking an interest in the matter and are keeping a watch on what the committee is doing to justify its existence.

1st. Let me call Dr. McAll's attention to the fact that the so-called resolution, to which he refers in his letter as being found on page 104 of Vol. XIX of the Journal, is part of a paper prepared by his colleague, Dr. Gillison, and read before the Medical Conference in February, 1905. This was never made part of the official acts of the Conference, but simply came as a suggestion of what the writer thought was a desirable course to take. The official action of the Conference, which resulted in the appointment of the Publication Committee, and under which that committee is now acting, is found on pages 43 and 44 of Vol. XIX; the report of the committee which was appointed to take the matter into consideration being finally adopted as follows:

(1) We recommend to the Association that it undertakes the publication of a standard series of textbooks in Chinese, and when practicable a Chinese medical journal.

(2) That a Publication Committee be appointed, composed of the following members: (Here follow the names of the Committee).

(3) That of the surplus funds of the Association now in hand and at the end of each year, four-fifths be at the disposal of the committee, which shall also be em-

powered to raise funds by voluntary subscription for its work; such funds to be paid into the treasury of the Association.

No instructions further than the above have ever been given to the committee that I am aware of. We quite agree, however, with Dr. McAll that the method which he favors would be an excellent one if it were possible to put it in practice, namely for the committee to go over carefully the whole field of medical text-books published in America and England and select the best of the lot, and then appoint men to translate these selected books. But unfortunately the work of this committee is wholly voluntary, and has to be done in the intervals of other work. No member of the committee can devote one quarter of his time to the work connected with this publication business, nor has the committee any power to compel men to do work which it thinks desirable to have done, nor has it funds to pay the expenses of meeting from time to time to consult about what is best to do.

Under the circumstances the only feasible thing seemed to be to accept for publication any books which were offered, and which were approved by the Executive and Editorial Sub-Committee, and to see what could be done with existing books in the way of revision and republication. It was deemed an eminently wise thing to approach the Canton Medical Missionary Society in regard to being allowed to revise and reissue some of their books—in fact we first thought of buying them out entirely, but failed to come to terms—for, as everyone knows, the Books issued in Canton have a sale all over the empire, and while some are not at all what we would desire to introduce into a standard series, others, such as *Practice*, are excellent books and have served a most useful purpose in training medical students during the past twenty years or more. So if these more useful ones can be revised and brought down to date, and thus preserve the old and yet introduce what is necessary to make them fit for present-day use, would it not seem a wise thing to do? The Canton people have agreed to allow us to select any of their books we wish to, and after revising them publish them under our imprimatur, with the understanding that they receive fifty per cent, of the net profits. So far only Dr. Kerr's *Practice* has been selected for such revision.

2nd. Dr. Cousland's translation of *Osier*, while originally suggested by himself, met the hearty approval of the committee, as there never has been a question that *Osier* is an excellent book, the best apparently that the members of the committee were acquainted with. No doubt others might have individual preferences, just as Dr. McAll has for Taylor, and if we could get together and compare notes, possibly we might select a better book than Osier, but it is rather disconcerting to find the committee blamed for selecting such a standard book as the one agreed upon.

3rd. No decision whatever has been made as to a general surgery, so that the field is open for suggestions. There is, however, no thought whatever of trying to revise Kerr's *Surgery*, one of the poorest of the Canton series. The only book which the committee has on its list in this line is Dr. Main's translation of *Caird and Cathcart's Surgical Handbook*, and even this has not been finally passed upon, as Dr. Main has been too busy to get it into shape to show the committee for criticism.

4th. Finally I may say in closing that the following are the only books so far that the committee has finally accepted and that are either already published or in press:

1. Couslaud's *Physiology*, a translation of Haliburton's.
2. Ingrain's *Therapeutics*, a translation of Hare and Wood.
3. Fulton's *Diseases of Women*, a translation of Penrose.
4. Niles' *Obstetrics*, a translation of Evans, etc.
5. Neal's *Diseases of the Eye*.
6. Neal's *Diseases of the Skin*.
7. Niles' *Revision of Kerr's Practice*.

Venable's *Bacteriology* and Cousland's translation of *Osier* have been agreed to by the committee, but are not yet in press, nor will they be until after the next meeting of the Association. *The Manual of Nursing*, translated in Hankow, has been presented to the Association, but was never passed upon by its committee. There will be an opportunity for the Association to discuss at its coming meeting in April the work of its Publication Committee, and we trust a full and free discussion will take place, and that the committee may be greatly helped by practical suggestions as to what the Association thinks it wise to attempt in the way of getting out a standard series of medical text-books in Chinese.

Truly yours,

James B. Neal

Chairman, Publication Committee

聂会东夫人写给倪维思(Nevius)夫人的信件

摘　录

首先说一下你曾问过的我们尊贵的朋友姜(Chiang)氏家族。

姜老夫人总是对外国人充满了恐惧和不信任;但她的两个儿子曾在通商口岸和北京待过,吸收了一些当地社会缺乏的文明思想。他们长期以来一直是济南府许多医学传教士的朋友,并且经常会面。

去年,聂会东医生缓解了他们年迈老父亲的皮肤疾病造成的痛苦,消除了他对外国人的偏见。

过去的3年里,老太太的双眼患有白内障,而且几乎完全丧失了视力。她的儿子们劝她去找聂会东医生,但几个月来她都不同意。之后他们多次去医院,要求观看白内障手术,并向他们胆小的母亲报告治疗方法。他们还把病人在手术前和手术后都分别带到家里见他们的父母。

最后,经过几个月的好言相劝,老太太同意来让聂会东医生看看她的眼睛是否可以通过手术治好,但她只答应让他检查一下。

那天下午,我碰巧在诊所,老太太坐在椅子上,身边有四位随从和他的儿子,在男病人角了解相关事宜。她“浑身颤抖”,可怜的老人,后来她告诉我,她的心里忐忑不安,心跳得就像是挥动的杵锤一样。她发现她能理解我所说的话,我穿着的中国服装,我的手和脸使她立刻忘记了恐惧,并以最坦诚的方式和我交谈。后来,当聂会东医生走进来,她发现他也可以与他交流,尤其是当他请求她不要害怕他的时候,她的胆怯就完全消失了,取而代之的是一种亲切感。

在我们看来,她是一位温柔、优雅的女士,声音甜美,举止娴静。她的两个儿子很孝顺她,顺道是中国广为推崇的儒家所倡导的伦理道德。

当她后来一只眼睛做手术的时候,两个儿子都和她一起来了;虽然她有许多仆人，但在头 3 个星期里，他的儿子对她寸步不离，日夜守在她身边。起初她的眼睛预后很好，但是她受到惊吓，在夜里，她顶在房门上的椅子被风吹倒了。她受到了深深的惊吓，以至于把第二天出现的炎症归因于此。

情况持续严重，以至于大家有一阵担心手术失败了。不过，虽然还不够理想，但她看东西比治疗前好多了。她现在可以看到大的字、她房间里的东西等等。

和我们在一起 5 周后回家，她和我成了很好的朋友，她给我送了两件礼物。第一件是丝绸毛皮内衬的衣服，说什么也要让我们收下。她还送聂会东医生一件丝绸毛皮衬里的“马褂”。她的儿子正在跟我学英语。他又有了一个“学位”，并将在明年夏天获得官方职位，他 37 岁了，非常聪明。

至于信奉基督教。她的儿子理解得很透彻，但我担心他们认为信奉基督教会阻碍在政治上的晋升，因为这个原因也不会对耶稣公开忏悔。

但是，姜老夫人两次告诉我，他们在她的房间里早晚向上帝祈祷，并补充说：“你不要认为我们会在回家后放弃它。”她说她不应该再崇拜其他神像、烧纸或焚香。我真的觉得有些光就像进入她可怜的眼睛一样，进入了她的心。

当她的眼睛状况恶化，我们都感到很失望的时候，尤其是在最初几天绷带被移除她能看到儿子们的脸而感到喜悦之后，她的儿子去了我们的新教堂，找到教堂司事，让他打开教堂，然后进去祈祷他母亲的眼睛能完全恢复。这难道不令人感动吗？他带着一个小基督徒，对他说：“你也跪下来祈祷我母亲的眼睛能治好。”这个小男孩告诉我，他是那么虔诚，那么真诚。难道你不认为这样的请愿一定会感动我们有爱心、有同情心的主吗？

我们希望她在这只眼睛完全康复后，再做另一只眼睛的手术。可能会由于恢复缓慢，她今年春天不再过来。等到炎热的天气过去，秋天到来时，她应该会过来手术。

简单说一下学习班的情况吧。10 位妇女在这里进行为期 2 个月的学习。自从 1893 年从美国回来以后，我每年冬天都办这样的学习班。

我们给妇女提供食物，同时给予单程旅费。住在城里的居民则只来接受教导。这次只有 2 人，其他几年，班级人数相当多。我们的想法是让同样的女性每年都来，当她们回家的时候，教那些（对基督教）了解甚少的人。如果她们没有表现出帮助其他人的意愿，她们的名字将不会出现在来年开课前发出的名单上。以这种方式，我们教会了许多女性教义、福音书、旧约和新约历史以及天路历程，她们反过来又帮助更多的人学习圣经。明年冬天，我希望可以用到你的“毅力”和“Hung-shin-shiu-tao”，这样你也可以教她们了。我经常希望能拥有你那样教人唱诗的天赋。在这个领域，她们确实发出了可怕的噪音！

今年，我每天下午都要花很长的时间教中国人文字，导致用眼过度。所以在我整个 6 周的假期里，我不得不让眼睛休息。我本来是打算进行大量的阅读和写作的啊！但是休息让我的眼睛更强壮了，也让我更加能“胜任”春天将要开展的工作。

我上午的时间在男孩学校，下午的时间进行英语教学以及与诊所的女患者谈话。

我从来没有感到这样令人鼓舞的前景。但是啊，还有好多工作等待着我。

(摘自 *Women's Work in the Far East*, 1895, 16(5)]

From Chinan Fu: An Extract from a Letter from Mrs, J. B. Neal to Mrs. Nevius

FIRST about our aristocratic friends, the Chiang family, of whom you asked me.

The old lady had always had the usual amount of dread and distrust of foreigners; but her two sons had been at the treaty ports and in Peking, and had imbibed some idea of the possibility of there being a civilization not altogether lacking in letters, and especially in science. They have long been friends of the different medical missionaries in Chinan Fu, and have been treated not infrequently by them.

Last year their old father had his prejudices removed in the same way, when Dr. Neal was able to relieve a painful skin disease.

For three years past the lao t'ai-t'ai has had cataracts growing in both eyes, and gradually had lost her sight almost altogether. Her sons urged her to come to Dr. Neal; but for months she wouldn't hear to it. They then visited the hospital constantly, and always asked to be allowed to witness the operations for cataract, reporting the cures to their timid mother. Next they had patients taken to their home for their parents to see both before and again after the operations.

Finally, after months of "good words", as the Chinese say, the old lady consented to come to let Dr. Neal see if her eyes could be cured by an operation, but she would only promise to let him look at them.

I happened in at the dispensary that afternoon just after she had arrived in her chair with four attendants besides her son, who was received of course in the men's quarter. She was "all of a tremble", poor old soul, and her heart, she told me afterwards, was going like a trip-hammer. Somehow when she found she could understand me, and that I had on a Chinese garment she felt it, my hands and face she immediately forgot her fear and talked with me in the frankest manner possible. Then when Dr. Neal came in and turned out also to be an intelligible human being, and especially when he begged her not to fear him, the timidity vanished utterly, and was replaced with a feeling of affectionate regard.

She is a lady, in our sense of the word, gentle, refined and of sweet voice and quiet manner. Her two sons are devoted to her after the most approved Confucian type of filial piety.

When she came later for the operation upon one eye the sons both came with her; and, though she had a number of servants with her, they did not leave her side, night nor day, for the first three weeks. At first her eye did well. Then she had a fright, caused by the falling of a heavy chair against her door in the night, the wind having blown it over. That startled her so much that she attributes to the incident the inflammation which began next day.

It was so continued and severe that it was feared for a while the operation would turn out a failure. But though not yet well she can see much better than before it was treated. She can now see large characters, the objects in her room, etc.

She and I became very good friends, and since her return home, after being five weeks with us, she has sent me presents twice. Once a silk fur-lined circular, and nothing would do but we must accept it. She also sent Dr. Neal a silk fur-lined "ma-kua". Her son is learning English with me. He has a second "degree", and is to have official position given him next summer. He is 37 years old, and very bright.

As for their embracing Christianity. The sons understand it well intellectually, but I fear they think its acceptance would hinder promotion politically, and will not for that reason think of an open confession of Christ.

But Mrs. Chiang told me twice that they prayed in her room night and morning to the Heavenly Father, and added, "You mustn't think we will give it up on our return home." She said she should never again worship idols or burn paper or incense. I really think some light had as truly entered her heart as her poor eyes.

When her eye was very bad, and when we all felt so disappointed particularly after the joy she had had the first few days of seeing her sons' faces when the bandages were removed her son went over to our new Church, hunted up the sexton, had him open up the building and went in to pray for the full recovery of his mother's eye. Wasn't it pathetic? He took a little Christian lad with him and said, "You kneel too and pray that my mother's eye may be healed." This boy told me how reverent he had been, how earnest and sincere. Don't you think such petitions must be pleasing to the all-loving and compassionate Father of us all?

We expect them to return for an operation on the other eye as soon as this eye becomes thoroughly well. It may be, as it is recovering very slowly, that she cannot come back this spring. Then she will wait until alter the hot weather is over and come in the autumn.

A few words about the class. Ten women were here for two months study. I have had such classes every winter since our return from America in 1893.

We give food to the women and traveling money one way. Those who live here in the city and attend receive only their instruction. There were but two such this time, other years the class has been rather larger. Our idea is to have the same women come each year, and they, when they go home, teach those who know less. If they do not show an inclination to be helpful to others, their names are not on the list that is sent out each year before the class opens. In this way we have taught a number of women the Catechism, Gospels, Old and New Testament History and Pilgrim's Progress, and they in turn have helped many more in their study of the Bible. Next winter I hope to use your "Perseverance", " Hung-shin-shiu-tao", so you will be teaching them too. I often and often wish I had your gift of teaching these women to sing. They do make such horrible noises in this part of the mission field.

This year I overtaxed my eyes teaching Chinese characters too long each afternoon, so that during my whole six weeks' holiday I have had to rest them almost all of the time. I had meant to do so much reading and writing! But I am rewarded by having my eyes much stronger as well as feeling very "fit" myself for the spring work which is just about opening.

The boys' school is to occupy the morning, and my English teaching and talking with women patients at the dispensary the afternoon.

Never, we think, has the prospect here been so encouraging. But oh! The amount of work to be done.

附　　录

聂会东大事纪年表

1855 年 5 月 8 日，出生于宾夕法尼亚州布鲁斯伯格镇(Bloomsburg)。

1877 年，毕业于耶鲁大学。

1877～1879 年，在纽黑文市的耶鲁大学谢菲尔德科技学院(Sheffield Scientific School)学习医学预科课程。

1879 年，在宾州丹维尔 (Danville)的第一国家银行学习金融和经商，同时跟从斯特劳布里奇医生(Dr. James D. Strawbridge)见习医学知识。

1880 年～1883 年 5 月，在宾夕法尼亚大学医学院学习。

1883 年 8 月 8 日，与伊丽莎白・西蒙顿 (Elizabeth B. Simonton) 在马里兰州的埃米茨堡 (Emmitsburg) 结婚。

1883 年 11 月 27 日，携夫人来到中国山东登州，居住在狄考文家中；并在登州文会馆、登州长老会医院从事教学、医疗和传教工作。

1887 年，在登州东大寺开展医学教育，教授 5 名学生。

1888 年，开始从事中药研究，在登州研究 16 种天然药物，分析化学成分并撰写《十六种天然无机药物》加以记述。

1889 年，撰写《子宫清理手术》《回归热》《1888 年登州府医疗工作报告》《论医学生培养及其成功前景》。

1890 年，根据教会安排前往济南工作。

1892～1893 年，回美国休假。

1892 年 8 月，文壁医院修建完工。

1893 年秋～1894 年春，主持文壁医院扩建。

1894 年，医院新建医学生楼，文壁医校招收 12 名学生。总结在山东开展医学工作的情况，成文《山东的医学工作》。

1895 年，参加在潍县举办的年度传教士会议；发表《医学传教士的科研机会》一文。

1897 年，医校 10 名学生毕业，另有 5 名学生在读；发表文章：《中国医学教育现状》，翻译出版《化学辨质》。

1898 年，主持确定“眼科术语”的命名，5 月 12 日回美国休假。

1898 年～1900 年，前往芝罘代替芝罘海关的莫利纽克斯医生（Dr. Molyneux）处理海关和其他事务。

1901 年，返回济南工作；拜访时任山东巡抚的袁世凯，并为其母亲治病。

1900～1922 年，任中国医学术语命名委员会委员，致力于出版翻译科学书籍和专业术语命名的规范化，翻译出版了《眼科证治》《皮肤证治》。

1903 年～1905 年，任中华博医会主席。

1904 年，在全国各地传教团体中开展中国医疗数据调查；3 月 1 日，主持在上海举行的博医会会员大会。

1905 年，发表文章《文璧医院》，对文璧医院的建立及发展做了回顾；发表文章《中国博医会》，总结博医会成立以来的成就与不足，对以后的工作进行展望。

1907 年，受邀参观北京医学院，认为不适合将山东的学生送到北京去学习；写信对出版委员会的工作提出几点建议。

1909 年，为在济南建立联合医科大学做准备工作；发表《济南联合医科大学》一文，详细阐述了大学建立的原因及创办计划。

1910～1919 年，任齐鲁大学医学院的院长。

1910 年 2 月，出席博医会在汉口的会议，作《如何激发医学生的科学兴趣》的报告，并参与了一些议案的讨论。

1911～1912 年，肺鼠疫大流行期间，因在拯救生命和控制疫情上做出了巨大的贡献，被中国政府授予“仓廪”（Garnered Grain）勋章。

1915 年，撰写关于中国膳食中主要食物价值研究的论文，发表文章《中国的联合医科大学》。

1918 年，在美国长老教会山东差会 1918 年 7 月 8 日在登州举办的年会上当选为山东差会主席。

1919 年 8 月 22 日，参加山东差会的年会，卸任山东差会主席。

1919～1921 年，担任齐鲁大学校长。

1921 年 1 月，因病不能视事，提出辞去校长职务请求。

1922 年，差会同意其辞职请求，聂会东返回费城。

1925 年 2 月 4 日，逝世于费城。

1939 年 8 月 4 日，妻子伊丽莎白·西蒙顿在宾夕法尼亚州匹兹堡逝世。

中英文地名对照表

山东 Shantung

济南府 Chinanfu/Chinan Fu

济南 Tsinan

登州府 Tengchowfu/ Tung-chow Fu

沂州府 Ichowfu

青州府 Tsing-chowfu/ Chingchow Fu

济宁州 Chining Chow

保定府 Paoting Fu

漳州府 Changchow Fu

潮州府 Chaochow Fu

邹平 Chouping

潍县 Wei Hien

芝罘 Chefoo

北京 Peking

通州 Tungchow

天津 Tientsin

奉天 Mukeden

成都 Chengtu

汉口 Hankow

鼓岭 Kuling

南京 Nanking

苏州 Soochow

杭州 Hangchow

福州 Foochow

广州 Canton

四川 Szechuan

满洲里 Manchuria

重庆 Chungking

孝感 Sioke

金华 Kinhwa

汕头 Swaton

永春 Eng-chhun

平度 Pingtu

锦州 Chinchow

中英文人名对照表

聂会东 James Boyed Neal
武成献 James Russell Watson
巴德顺 Thomas C. Paterson
洪士提凡 Stephen A. Hunter
章嘉礼 Charles F. Johnson
冯夏克 I. L. Van Schoick
李佳白 Gibert Reid
库寿龄 Samuel Couling
郭显德 Hunter Corbett
梅藤更 David Duncan Main
嘉约翰 John Glasgow kerr
阿撒拉 Sarah Archibalol Mateer
吉佛瑞 William Hamilton Jefferys
文恒理 Herry William Boone
高似兰 Philip B. cousland
惠亨通 Henry T. Whitney
孟合理 Percy Lonsdale McAll
纪立生 Thomas Gillison
赖马西 Mary West Niles
富玛利 Mary fulton
盈亨利 James Henry Ingram
韩维廉 William Beeson Hamilton
莫约翰 John Murray
倪维思 Heler S. C. Nevius